best hikes with KIDS

OREGON

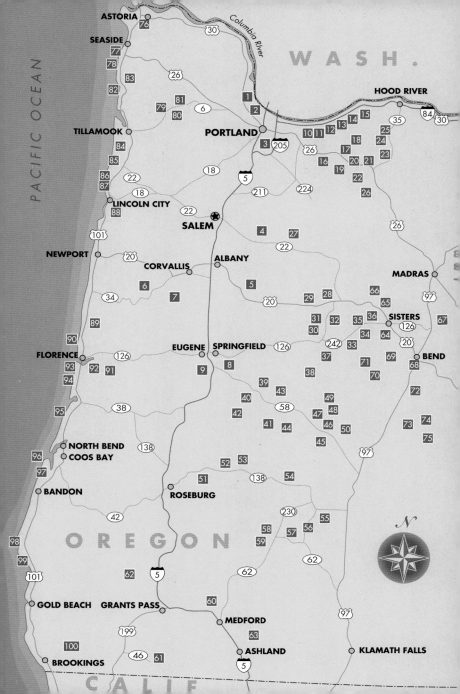

best hikes with KIDS
OREGON

917.95
HENDERS
2007

Bonnie Henderson

THE MOUNTAINEERS BOOKS

"If a child is to keep alive his inborn sense of wonder . . . he needs the companionship of at least one adult who can share it, rediscovering with him the joy, excitement, and mystery of the world we live in."
— Rachel Louise Carson, from *The Sense of Wonder*
(Harper and Row, 1965)

THE MOUNTAINEERS BOOKS
is the nonprofit publishing arm of The Mountaineers Club, an organization founded in 1906 and dedicated to the exploration, preservation, and enjoyment of outdoor and wilderness areas.

1001 SW Klickitat Way, Suite 201, Seattle, WA 98134

© 2007 by Bonnie Henderson

Previous edition published as *Best Hikes with Children: Western and Central Oregon,* 2nd edition.

Manufactured in the United States of America

Cover and Book Design: The Mountaineers Books
Page 2 photo: © Morgue File
Page 4 photo: © Phaedra Wilkinson
Page 30 photo: © *www.dreamstime.com*
Photos pages 1, 18, 25, 27, and 31 © Margaret Sullivan
All photos by the author unless otherwise noted above.
All illustrations by Barbara Gleason except illustration on page 46 is © The Mountaineers Books and illustration on page 193 is from *Mountaineering: Freedom of the Hills. 7th ed*. Seattle: The Mountaineers Books, 2003. Cox, Steven M., and Kris Fulsaas, eds.
Cover photograph: © Veer

Library of Congress Cataloging-in-Publication Data
Henderson, Bonnie.
  Best hikes with kids in Oregon / author Bonnie Henderson.—1st ed.
    p. cm.
  Includes index.
  1. Hiking—Oregon—Guidebooks. 2. Family recreation—Oregon—
Guidebooks. 3. Oregon—Guidebooks. I. Title.
GV199.42.O7H463 2007
796.5109795—dc22
                                    2006030381

 Printed on recycled paper

CONTENTS

ACKNOWLEDGMENTS

Thanks to all the national forest and state parks personnel who have offered advice on trails, based on both their professional knowledge and their personal experience with their own children. Thanks to all the friends who have taken on the tough duty of accompanying me on hikes. Thanks to my very encouraging family, especially Charlie.

A NOTE ABOUT SAFETY

Safety is an important concern in all outdoor activities. No guidebook can alert you to every hazard or anticipate the limitations of every reader. Therefore, the descriptions of roads, trails, routes, and natural features in this book are not representations that a particular place or excursion will be safe for your party. When you follow any of the routes described in this book, you assume responsibility for your own safety. Under normal conditions, such excursions require the usual attention to traffic, road and trail conditions, weather, terrain, the capabilities of your party, and other factors. Keeping informed on current conditions and exercising common sense are the keys to a safe, enjoyable outing.

—The Mountaineers Books

KEY TO SYMBOLS

 Day hikes. These are hikes that can be completed in a single day. While most trips allow camping, few require it.

 Backpack trips. These are hikes to remote locations with good campsites, allowing overnighting as well as day hiking.

 Easy trails. These are relatively short, smooth, gentle trails suitable for small children or first-time hikers.

 Moderate trails. Most of these feature more than 500 feet of elevation gain. The trails may be rough and uneven. Hikers should wear lug-soled boots and be sure to carry the Ten Essentials.

 Challenging trails. These are often rough and involve considerable elevation gain or distance. They are suitable for older or experienced children. Lug-soled boots and the Ten Essentials are standard equipment.

   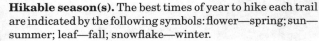 **Hikable season(s).** The best times of year to hike each trail are indicated by the following symbols: flower—spring; sun—summer; leaf—fall; snowflake—winter.

A QUICK GUIDE TO THE HIKES

Use this guide to quickly home in on a hike you'll like. The hikes are grouped by location and listed in order of difficulty (E for easy, M for moderate, C for challenging). (Note that some numbered hike descriptions may include options of varying difficulty.) To pick a hike:

- Glance over the region where you intend to hike.
- Narrow your choices to those of the difficulty level you seek.
- Make sure the trail is accessible now (season).
- Look over the highlights to get a sense of the hike.

Turn to the full hike description for distance, elevation gained, and other specifics. Enjoy your outing!

NUMBER AND NAME	DIFFICULTY	SEASON	HIGHLIGHTS
Willamette Valley			
1. Virginia Lake	E	Year-round	Birds, boats, pastures on a quiet island
2. Oak Island	E	Mid-April–September	Island on an island with birds and oak groves
3. Tryon Creek	E	Year-round	Forest and creek in the city, with early spring wildflowers
5. McDowell Creek Falls	E	Year-round	Three waterfalls, lots of bridges, pretty woods
6. Marys Peak Summit	E	April–November	Summit hike to great views, summer wildflowers
6. Marys Peak Meadowedge Trail	E	April–November	Great views, summer wildflowers, deep woods
7. Woodpecker Loop	E	Year-round	Mixed forest and open swales on a Canada goose refuge
8. Mount Pisgah: Water Garden	E	Year-round	Riverside trail to a turtle pond
6. Marys Peak North Ridge Loop	M	April–November	Deep woods and wildflowers
4. Silver Falls	M–C	Year-round	Ten major waterfalls in a stunning canyon
8. Mount Pisgah: Summit	M–C	Year-round	Summit hike to great views, forest and meadow
9. Spencer Butte	M–C	Year-round	Deep forest hike to great summit views
Columbia Gorge and Mount Hood			
11. Bridal Veil Falls	E	Most of the year	Easy waterfall walk
13. Horsetail Falls–Oneonta Falls	E	Most of the year	Waterfalls, a scenic gorge, early spring wildflowers
14. Wahclella Falls	E	Most of the year	Bridges and boardwalk to waterfalls
16. Cascade Streamwatch	E	Most of the year	Intriguing interpretive displays along wetland and river
17. Lost Creek	E	May–October	Accessible trail along a lush mountain creek
19. Old Salmon River Trail	E	Most of the year	Level trail among big trees along clear mountain river

Hike		Season	Description
21. Little Zigzag Falls	E	April–November	Accessible walk to a musical waterfall
23. Timberline Trails: White River Canyon Overlook	E	July–October	Alpine scenery and late summer wildflowers
26. Little Crater Lake	E	May–October	Accessible trail to jewel-like pond, summer wildflowers
10. Latourell Falls	E–M	Most of the year	Waterfalls and early spring wildflowers
12. Multnomah Falls	M	Most of the year	Walk to the top of the state's most famous waterfall
15. Eagle Creek: Punch Bowl Falls	M	Most of the year	Scenic canyon and impressive waterfall
19. Salmon River	M	Most of the year	Wilderness trail with river access
22. Mirror Lake	M	May–October	Forest hike to picture-postcard lake, summer wildflowers
23. Timberline Trails: Zigzag Canyon Overlook	M	July–October	Alpine scenery and late summer wildflowers
24. Umbrella Falls–Sahalie Falls	M	June–October	Alpine forest, high meadows, waterfalls
25. Tamawanas Falls	M	May–October	Mossy stream, footbridges, waterfall
20. Hidden Lake	M–C	May–October	Quiet forest lake on Mount Hood's slope
15. Eagle Creek: High Bridge	C	Most of the year	Scenic canyon and waterfalls
18. Ramona Falls	C	May–October	Lacy waterfall, mossy creek, rushing glacier-fed river
Northern Cascades			
33. Proxy Falls	E	July–October	Easy walk to two waterfalls
35. Hand Lake	E	July–October	Forest and high meadow hike to small lake
41. Spirit and Moon Falls	E	Most of the year	Easy walks to two waterfalls
46. Marilyn Lakes	E	July–October	Two lakes and easily reached campsite
49. Islet Beach	E	July–October	Lake views and easy hike to camping, cool swimming
38. East Fork McKenzie	E–M	Most of the year	Deep forest, creek, footbridges
39. Fall Creek	E–M	Year-round	Creekside walking through deep forest and burn, swimming holes

NUMBER AND NAME	DIFFICULTY	SEASON	HIGHLIGHTS
43. North Fork Trail	E–M	Year-round	Quiet, scenic riverside trail
44. Larison Cove	E–M	Year-round	Forest hike with old-growth trees to remote reservoir arm
48. South Waldo Shelter	E–M	July–October	Lake views, camping along scenic Waldo Lake
42. Brice Creek	E–C	Most of the year	Creekside walking, short or long
27. Opal Creek (to Cascada de los Niños)	M	Most of the year	Ancient forest of huge trees, waterfall and rushing river
30. Tamolitch Pool	M	Most of the year	Forest walk on McKenzie River to turquoise lake
31. Sahalie Falls–Koosah Falls	M	Most of the year	Two gushing waterfalls on forest loop
32. Clear Lake	M	Most of the year	Old-growth forest, lava flow, lake views
34. Linton Lake	M	July–October	Forest hike to mountain lake
35. Benson and Hand Lakes	M	July–October	Forest hike to mountain lakes
37. Horsepasture Mountain	M	July–October	Forest, alpine wildflower meadows, summit peak views
40. Goodman Creek	M	Year-round	Forest hike to a small creek
45. Salt Creek Falls–Diamond Creek Falls	M	June–October	High mountain loop hike to large and small waterfalls
47. Bobby Lake	M	July–October	Nearly level forest walk to swimmable mountain lake
28. Echo Basin	M–C	July–October	Unusual old-growth forest, alpine meadow with boardwalk
27. Opal Creek (to Opal Pool or Jawbone Flats)	C	Most of the year	Ancient forest of huge trees, stunning creek, old mining camp
29. Iron Mountain	C	July–October	Steep hike with summer wildflowers, ending with view of Cascade peaks
36. Little Belknap Crater	C	July–October	Walk across a lava flow and up an old volcano

42. Brice Creek: Upper Trestle Creek Falls	C	Most of the year	Steep hike, then walk behind a waterfall
50. Rosary Lakes	C	July–October	Forest hike to exceptional string of mountain lakes
Southern Cascades and Siskiyous			
51. Fern Falls	E	Year-round	Easy waterfall hike with spring wildflowers
52. Susan Creek Falls	E	Year-round	Easy waterfall hike with spring wildflowers
53. Fall Creek Falls	E	Year-round	Easy waterfall hike with spring wildflowers
54. Toketee and Watson Falls	E	Most of the year	Dramatic waterfall views on easy hike
58. Natural Bridge	E	April–November	Geologic mystery and scenic riverside trail
56. The Watchman	E-M	July–October	Hike up to a lookout tower on the rim of Crater Lake
57. Union Creek	E-M	April–November	Babbling creek, ancient trees, late spring wildflowers
62. Rainie Falls	E-M	Year-round	Rogue River rapids and waterfall
55. Cleetwood Cove	M	July–October	Hike to the water's edge at Crater Lake
59. Takelma Gorge	M	Most of the year	Hike along a dramatic stretch of the Upper Rogue River
60. Upper Table Rock	M	Year-round	Hike to the top of a tall rock mesa; spring wildflowers
61. Oregon Caves–Big Tree Loop	M	July–October	Big and bigger trees along a loop inside a national monument
63. Grizzly Peak	M	May–October	Hike through forest and recent burn to peak-top views
East of the Cascades			
67. Smith Rock: River Path	E	Most of the year	Watch rock climbers from level trail along Crooked River
68. Deschutes River South Canyon	E	May–November	Easy in-town hike through narrow river canyon to footbridge
71. Todd Lake	E	July–October	Circle a high mountain lake
72. Lava River Cave	E	May–mid-October	Walk through an underground lava tube

NUMBER AND NAME	DIFFICULTY	SEASON	HIGHLIGHTS
73. Paulina Creek Falls	E	June–October	Short hikes to waterfall in pine forest
75. Obsidian Flow	E	June–October	Walk a short trail across a mound of black glass
64. Little Three Creek Lake	E–M	July–October	Walk from one mountain lake to another, under dramatic bluffs
66. Metolius River	E–M	Most of the year	Nearly level riverside trails and a fish hatchery visit
69. Tumalo Falls	E–C	June–October	Big and bigger waterfalls and creekside hiking
74. Paulina Lake	E–C	June–October	Circle a big lake in a volcanic caldera
65. Black Butte	M–C	June–October	Walk up a cinder cone to a cluster of old fire lookouts
67. Smith Rock: Misery Ridge	C	Most of the year	Climb steep trail up landmark rock formation
70. Tumalo Mountain	C	July–October	Summit ascent with views of Mount Bachelor and other close peaks
The Coast and West Slope Coast Range			
76. Cathedral Tree Trail	E	Year-round	Hike to a huge Sitka spruce and the Astoria Column
80. University Falls	E	Most of the year	Short walk to Coast Range waterfall
85. Whalen Island	E	Year-round	Trail circles a forested island in an estuary
89. Cape Perpetua: Shoreline	E	Year-round	Tide-pooling, beach walking and spouting horn
89. Cape Perpetua: Giant Spruce	E	Year-round	Accessible trail to a huge spruce
90. Hobbit Beach	E	Year-round	Short trail to a hidden beach
97. South Slough: Big Cedar	E	Year-round	Gentle path to boardwalk though salt marsh
98. Port Orford Heads	E	Year-round	Dramatic views and intriguing history on tall headland
79. Wilson River Trail	E–M	Most of the year	Cross the river on an impressive footbridge to follow a riverside trail
81. Gales Creek Trail	E–M	Most of the year	Drop into a cool creek canyon not far from Portland

	E–M		
100. Redwood Nature Trail		Year-round	Redwoods and other trees in lush forest above Chetco River
78. Indian Beach to Ecola Point	M	Year-round	Walk along a bluff overlooking the Pacific
82. Cape Falcon	M	Year-round	Wind through deep woods to a remote, scenic headland
84. Cape Lookout	M	Year-round	Follow a finger of land jutting into the Pacific
87. Cascade Head	M	Year-round	Dramatic coastal views from a headland nature preserve
88. Drift Creek Falls	M	Year-round	High suspension footbridge by a forest waterfall
89. Cape Perpetua: Discovery Loop	M	Year-round	Vigorous walk up into coastal forest
90. China Creek Loop	M	Year-round	Loop through coastal forest and along creek leads to optional beach walk
91. Kentucky Falls	M	Most of the year	Descend through forest to a pair of waterfalls
92. Sweet Creek	M	Year-round	Boardwalks and trail follow creek flowing over sculpted rock
93. Waxmyrtle Trail	M	Year-round	Wildlife-watching along coastal estuary and beach
94. Oregon Dunes Overlook	M	Year-round	Hike over open dunes, through tree islands, to beach
96. Cape Arago	M	Year-round	Wildlife watching, formal gardens, remote shoreline views
97. South Slough: Hidden Creek	M	Year-round	Creekside descent to salt marsh viewpoint
97. South Slough: Interpretive Center Trail	M	Year-round	Forest, salt marsh trails in national estuarine reserve
77. Tillamook Head	M–C	Year-round	Follow Lewis and Clark's footsteps to top of headland
83. Neahkahnie Mountain	M–C	Year-round	Climb through forest and meadow to grand shoreline views
86. Harts Cove	C	mid-July–Dec.	Walk through deep woods to a remote cove high above the shoreline
95. John Dellenback Trail	C	Year-round	Adventurous hike over extensive shifting sand dunes
99. Humbug Mountain	C	Year-round	Ascend forested coastal mountain to grand shoreline views

INTRODUCTION

Two friends head to the beach.

WHY HIKE WITH CHILDREN?

They can get exercise at the gym, and they can learn about nature at a museum or interpretive center. Is hiking even necessary anymore?

Now more than ever, I'd say, and I have lots of company—among them, pediatricians, psychologists, physicists, biologists, and other parents.

"Children need contact with the natural world," writes Mary Pipher in *The Shelter of Each Other* (Putnam Adult, 1996). "It's an antidote to advertising and gives them a different perspective on the universe. Looking at the Milky Way makes most of us feel small and yet a part of something vast. Television, with its emphasis on meeting every need, makes people feel self-important and yet unconnected to anything greater than themselves."

Pipher's thoughts are echoed by evolutionary biologist Edward Wilson, who hypothesizes that human beings have a deep, genetically based need to connect with the rest of the natural world. Meeting this need, he says, may be as important to human health as forming close, personal relationships. And nearly two generations ago—before TV, before video games—scientist Rachel Carson drew similar conclusions in an article she published for parents entitled, "Help Your Child to Wonder" from *Lost Woods: The Discovered Writing of Rachel Carson*, by Rachel Carson and Linda Lear (Beacon Press 1998).

"What is the value of preserving and strengthening this sense of awe and wonder, this recognition of something beyond the boundaries of human existence? Is the exploration of the natural world just a pleasant way to pass the golden hours of childhood, or is there something deeper?

"I am sure there is something much deeper, something lasting and significant. Those who dwell, as scientists or laymen, among the beauties and mysteries of the earth are never alone or weary of life. . . . Those who contemplate the beauty of the earth find reserves of strength that will endure as long as life lasts."

Accustomed as many kids are to the instant gratification of electronic games, it's not always easy to get children out the door and onto a trail these days. (As a fourth-grader told Richard Louv, author of the eye-opening *Last Child in the Woods,* indoor play is more fun because "that's where all the electrical outlets are.") Some kids love the prospect of an hour or a day on a trail, but more reluctant young hikers will do their best to discourage you. Add to their whining the gear gathering, the arrangements required to bring friends along, the driving, the logistics, and it's easy to get discouraged.

So why do we drive sometimes an hour or more to spend not much more than an hour on a trail? It gets us out of the city. It gives us time together. It helps us stay healthy. (With the increase in obesity among youth, the current generation of children may end up with a shorter average lifespan than their parents.) Physicists have found that simply viewing the "fractal patterns" found in clouds and tree branches and other patterns in nature—even just in our peripheral vision—measurably lowers anxiety levels. And when the weather takes an unexpected turn and we wind up hunkering down, slogging uncomfortably in the rain for an hour, we learn that we are stronger and more capable than we thought, that our sense of humor needn't disappear when the going gets tough. And when we're back home, we have a great story to tell.

Despite the title, this book isn't just for children; it's for anyone looking for a wide range of interesting, doable hikes. In fact, it's not for kids at all. It's for the adults who go to the trouble of taking kids hiking, not necessarily every weekend, but every now and then; who round up the kids and their friends, gather the gear, pack the lunches and snacks, overcome their own inertia at the end of a busy week, and maintain enthusiasm when the kids' spirits are flagging. What your kids need more than this book is a day outdoors, anywhere, with *you.*

MAKING ALL YOUR HIKES "THE BEST"

I was lucky that my growing-up years were filled with trips into the wilderness. But looking back now, I place these adventures into two categories: tedious, goal-oriented hikes, or fun, exploratory hikes. The first category includes a slog up a steep scree slope on a blazing summer day and portions of a backpack trip in Idaho that I remember as too long and, again, too hot. The second category was pure magic: wandering awestruck in a cathedral-like old-growth forest, fording creeks on fallen logs, pursuing orange-bellied salamanders across the mossy forest floor, and backpacking into a hidden lake so full of trout we could pick the fish we'd have for dinner before we cast.

BEST HIKES IN WINTER

Virginia Lake, Hike 1
Oak Island, Hike 2
Tryon Creek, Hike 3
Woodpecker Loop, Hike 7
Mount Pisgah, Hike 8
Spencer Butte, Hike 9
East Fork McKenzie, Hike 38
Fall Creek, Hike 39

North Fork Trail, Hike 43
Fern Falls, Hike 51
Susan Creek Falls, Hike 52
Upper Table Rock, Hike 60
Wilson River Trail, Hike 79
*Plus coastal Hikes 76-78, 82-85,
   87-90, 92-100*

I hope this book helps you create more family outings that fall into that second category. The following approaches have helped other adults create memorable outings for kids. Try them on yours.

- **Remember that not all three-year-olds fit size three pajamas.** A child's readiness for hiking is just as variable. Your kids will let you know when they're ready for a new challenge.
- **No siblings? "Adopt" some.** The extra hassle of taking more children on a hike is generally outweighed by the greater level of cooperation and plain fun your child is likely to have with a friend or two along.
- **Assign an engine and a caboose and rotate these roles.** The child in front, setting the pace, enjoys the perks—and a taste of the responsibility—that come with leadership. The caboose has the important job of ensuring that no one falls far behind (and, in the process, can feel as important as the engine).
- **Take plenty of snacks—even for a half-hour outing.** Children need the energy boost, and snacks—carefully rationed—can help keep enthusiasm high.
- **Avoid electronics.** Cell phones, GPS devices, and electronic maps have their place, but they inevitably pull kids out of the moment and distract them from the natural world around them. If you carry a cell phone, turn it off and bury it at the bottom of your pack. Hiking with kids these days is as much about unplugging as anything else.
- **Be generous with praise.** It can do more to raise energy levels than all the granola bars in the world.
- **Balance new hikes with old favorites.** Children often enjoy returning to favorite spots; vary the experience by going in different seasons or at different times of day. Choose trails with special

attractions scattered at intervals; as your children grow, so may the distances they're willing and able to hike.

- **Be a tortoise, not always a hare.** Slowly, with a lot of stops to catch grasshoppers or poke under rocks, your tortoises will usually get there. They may balk if required to travel at your adult hare's pace.
- **Encourage a family wilderness ethic.** By pointing out indiscretions of other hikers—an empty pop can beside the trail, shortcuts worn between switchbacks—and explaining why your family doesn't do that, you enlist your children as conservationists before it occurs to them to cut across those switchbacks themselves.
- **Don't confuse family hikes with adult workouts.** Reaching target heart rate has little allure for children. When you're out with the kids, be willing to take it slow. Try getting in your workout, if it's important to you, before a family hike so you're not rushed and frustrated.
- **Remember your real goal.** Do you want to reach the summit of a particular mountain, or to nurture your children's curiosity and sense of adventure and instill a love of the outdoors that will last a lifetime? The patience you demonstrate while the kids tarry over a mysterious hole in the ground, or while they stop—again—to rest and snack will reward you many times over.

Spencer Butte

HOW TO USE THIS BOOK

Anything can spoil a hike, especially for youngsters new to the outdoors whose tolerance for cold, heat, fatigue, bugs, and even long car rides can be limited at best. A parent's first job is to choose trails carefully. I selected the hikes in this book for their appeal to kids and for their relative ease—children may go farther on a difficult, but interesting, trail than on a flat, but boring, trail. Most of the trails lie close to main roads and don't require a tedious drive on gravel logging roads. They were also chosen with an eye toward geographical balance. Hence, many excellent trails were omitted. This book offers only a selection of the most interesting, relatively short trails in western and central Oregon; it is in no way a definitive list.

Most of the trails included here go no farther than 1.5 miles without a treat of some kind: a waterfall, a bridge, a lake, a great view, a mountain of glass, or a tunnel of lava. That way, if hikers go no farther than this turnaround point, everyone can still come away with a sense of accomplishment. This guide steers away from view hikes that require a long uphill slog before offering any reward. By the time your child is ready to switchback 4 miles up a relatively uninteresting trail to reach a stellar viewpoint, you no longer need this book.

Young hikers enjoy the view.

BEST HIKES TO WATERFALLS

McDowell Creek Falls, Hike 5
Multnomah Falls, Hike 12
Horsetail Falls–Oneonta Falls, Hike 13
Wahclella Falls, Hike 14
Umbrella Falls–Sahalie Falls, Hike 24
Tamawanas Falls, Hike 25
Sahalie Falls–Koosah Falls, Hike 31
Salt Creek Falls–Diamond Creek Falls, Hike 45

Toketee and Watson Falls, Hike 54
Tumalo Falls, Hike 69
Kentucky Falls, Hike 91
Including three walk-behind waterfalls:
Silver Falls (South and North Falls), Hike 4
Brice Creek (Upper Trestle Creek Falls), Hike 42
For more waterfalls, check out Hikes 10, 11, 15, 18, 33, 41, 51, 52, 53, 62, and 73.

BEST HIKES TO SEE WILDFLOWERS

Tryon Creek (spring), Hike 3
Marys Peak (summer), Hike 6
Latourell Falls (spring), Hike 10
Horsetail Falls–Oneonta Falls (spring), Hike 13
Timberline Trails (summer), Hike 23
Umbrella Falls–Sahalie Falls (summer), Hike 24

Echo Basin (summer), Hike 28
Iron Mountain (summer), Hike 29
Horsepasture Mountain (summer), Hike 37
Susan Creek Falls (spring), Hike 52
Fall Creek Falls (spring), Hike 53
Upper Table Rock (spring), Hike 60

Hikes are grouped geographically, oriented to major population centers (or, in the case of the coast, natural geographic boundaries). Some hikes stand by themselves, but in most cases several hikes are clustered around a major highway, giving car campers several choices for day trips during a family vacation.

SELECTING A HIKE

Glance at the capsule descriptions at the beginning of each hike in the area you intend to visit. These provide a snapshot of the hike—once you know how to read them.

Type: All the hikes in this book are short enough to be enjoyed as day hikes, meaning one-day or partial-day outings. If a hike is listed as a day hike only (not "day hike or backpack"), that means that overnighting is impractical (due to rough terrain, lack of water, etc.), inadvisable (due to a delicate environment), or prohibited.

Difficulty: The designation of a trail as easy, moderate, or challenging for children takes into consideration the trail condition, elevation gain, and distance to the major destination. Often children can travel long distances on level trails, especially with interesting distractions along the way. Add some elevation gain and long stretches without much variation in scenery, and the fatigue level quickly goes up. If a short hike is what you're after, don't limit your choices to those designated "easy"; even a trail rated "challenging" may in fact be easy and full of interest for the first mile, making that section a good choice for beginning hikers. Add your own judgment to the formula as well; an exposed ridgeline trail that's a breeze on a balmy June day can quickly turn into a nightmare in blistering heat or persistent rain, especially with very young, tired, or inexperienced hikers.

BEST SUMMIT HIKES

Marys Peak, Hike 6
Mount Pisgah, Hike 8
Spencer Butte, Hike 9
Iron Mountain, Hike 29
Horsepasture Mountain, Hike 37

The Watchman, Hike 56
Upper Table Rock, Hike 60
Black Butte, Hike 65
Tumalo Mountain, Hike 70
Neahkahnie Mountain, Hike 83
Humbug Mountain, Hike 99

Distance: For each hike, the total mileage for the outing is listed. A round-trip hike is the total distance to the destination and back out or to complete a loop. One-way hikes are those with trailheads accessible by car at either end. With a shuttle car, you can make these one-way hikes in one direction only (most appealing when the hike is downhill); if you intend to walk from one end to the other and back without the shuttle car, hike mileage will double.

Elevation gain: This figure is an estimate of the total elevation rise on a given hike, whether it's to the top of a mountain, the return from a trip down to a lake basin or beach, or all the elevation gain on an up-and-down trail.

High point: This number indicates the height above sea level of the highest point on the trail section described. Use it as a clue to how cold or exposed the trail might be, or how early or late in the year it might open up.

Hikable: This line generally indicates the months the trail is snow-free in a typical year, though the actual hiking season will vary from

Forest hikes are magical.

year to year according to snowpack and weather conditions. In some cases road closures dictate the hike's seasonal accessibility.

BEST HIKES TO A (BRISK) SWIM

Tamolitch Pool, Hike 30
Fall Creek, Hike 39
Larison Cove, Hike 44
Bobby Lake, Hike 47

South Waldo Shelter, Hike 48
Islet Beach, Hike 49
Sweet Creek, Hike 92

WHAT TO TAKE
"My Own Pack!"

Particularly with younger children, offering a pack of their own to carry can add excitement to an outing. You don't have to put much in it—the less the better, at first—but you may find you get more cooperation from a child wearing a pack. It seems to signal that you consider the wearer

Dee Wright Observatory, McKenzie Pass

a bona fide member of the party, not just a youngster the adults brought along on their outing.

Small packs sized for children are widely available, but a smallish adult's day pack may get used for more years; just don't overload it. Children also love fanny packs. One woman I know adds something special to her grandchild's pack every time they hike: colorful adhesive bandages, a small flashlight, or an emergency whistle.

Boots or Shoes?

Boots used to be the standard footwear for hiking of any kind, but these days a good quality athletic shoe with support and a traction sole is considered quite adequate for most day hikes. If you plan to be on rough terrain, or in snow or on a very wet trail, or if you are carrying heavy packs, you may need more substantial footwear.

Look for boots made of pliable, split-grain leather or Gore-Tex (or a combination of the two), with a soft collar and treat them for water-repellency when recommended. Stiffer boots may require a breaking-in period; have children wear them around the house at first to make sure they fit, then around the neighborhood (for more than a few minutes) before embarking on a major outing. Then, just in case, carry moleskin and apply it at the first sign of discomfort. I've found that the best way to avoid blisters is to buy boots a half-size larger than your usual shoe size.

BEST HIKES TO BEACHES AND SAND DUNES

Cape Falcon (Short Sand Beach), Hike 82
Whalen Island, Hike 85
Hobbit Beach–China Creek, Hike 90

Waxmyrtle Trail, Hike 93
Oregon Dunes Overlook, Hike 94
John Dellenback Trail, Hike 95

Opposite: Oregon beaches offer toddlers a chance to get their feet wet.

THE TEN ESSENTIALS

You say you're planning to hike only 2 miles, and the weather's beautiful? It's still a good idea to make sure most, if not all, of the following items are in your day pack, especially when hiking with children. This list, compiled by The Mountaineers, has become an accepted standard for hikers and other recreationists.

1. **Extra clothing.** Not necessarily a complete set of clothes, but do take at least one more sweater than you think you'll need and, on all but the best summer days, raingear. Extra socks are a good idea. Take lightweight water shoes if you plan to do much wading.

2. **Extra food.** Pack what you plan to eat—and then some, just in case. The traditional hiker's menu consists of high-energy, noncrushable foods that won't spoil too quickly, such as dried fruits, nuts, hard crackers, cheese and dried meats, and—in limited quantity—candy. Fresh fruit is heavier but refreshing. Pick foods your children don't ordinarily get, or save certain treats for outings (dried fruit rolls or boxed juices, for example), to make hikes special.

3. **Sunglasses.** Children of hiking age usually like to wear shades, especially if they've helped to pick them out. Encouraging kids to wear sunglasses now (especially if they're around water and snow) helps reduce their chances of developing cataracts years down the road.

4. **Knife.** One with various blades and gadgets is particularly useful (for adults, and eventually for whittling kids).

5. **Fire starter.** A candle or chemical fire starter of some kind adds little weight to the pack and can be a lifesaver if you wind up bivouacking unexpectedly.

6. **First-aid kit.** Keep it supplied with the basics, plus any special medications your group requires such as a bee sting kit if someone is allergic.

7. **Matches.** Waterproof matches, available at sporting goods stores, are the safest; in any case, keep them in a secure, waterproof container. An inexpensive lighter or two are also handy to keep in a pack.

8. **Flashlight.** Tiny, light, but powerful minilights are widely available.

9. **Map.** Many of the trails in this book aren't so isolated or complicated that they require a map for routefinding, though it's always a good idea to carry one. Older children may enjoy learning to read maps in the field. Maps are often necessary for finding your way on the sometimes complicated network of roads leading to national forest trailheads.

10. **Compass.** Be sure to learn how to use it with a map.

What's Not Among the Ten Essentials?

Electronic games, maps, and GPS devices. They're fun and can be helpful, but they tend to distract kids from what's right around them. One reason for hiking is to unplug, for at least a little while.

Cell phone. It can be handy, even life-saving. But you may not have service when you need it. And in an emergency you will still have to wait for help to arrive. Make sure you have all the other Ten Essentials with you before packing a cell phone. Turn it off, bury it at the bottom of your pack, and please use it only for outgoing calls in an emergency (the rest of us on the summit don't want to hear your end of a cell phone conversation while we enjoy the view).

Making a rubbing on sighting pedestal, Mount Pisgah

BEST HIKES TO OLD-GROWTH FORESTS AND BIG TREES

Marys Peak, Hike 6
Salmon River, Hike 19
Opal Creek, Hike 27
Echo Basin, Hike 28
Tamolitch Pool, Hike 30
Fall Creek, Hike 39
Larison Cove, Hike 44

Oregon Caves–Big Tree Loop, Hike 61
Cathedral Tree, Hike 76
Tillamook Head, Hike 77
Harts Cove, Hike 86
Cascade Head, Hike 87
Redwood Nature Trail, Hike 100

SAFETY

It's easy to be lulled into complacency by a sunny day, a good trail, and your own physical strength and feeling of competence. But as anyone with any experience knows, the wilderness can be a dangerous place for the unprepared; conditions can change quickly, and accidents do sometimes happen. You can reduce your chances of disaster by covering two bases. First, be prepared. Learn something about the area you'll be going into and carry adequate emergency supplies. In classes or on the trail with more experienced companions, learn survival skills, including how to use a map and compass. Second, know your own limits and those of your party, and respect them.

All the trails in this guide have been field-checked, but conditions and routes change. The trail ratings (easy, moderate, and challenging) are estimations: Use them as guidelines, not as fact. Use your own best judgment to keep your party safe.

WEIRDEST HIKES

Little Crater Lake (but not really a crater), Hike 26
Tamolitch Pool (to a mysterious lake), Hike 30
Little Belknap Crater (across a lava flow), Hike 36
Natural Bridge (to a disappearing river), Hike 58
Grizzly Peak (through a burned forest), Hike 63
Lava River Cave (underground), Hike 72
Obsidian Flow (on a mountain of glass), Hike 75
Drift Creek Falls (to a suspension footbridge), Hike 88

Keeping up with an older sister on the trail.

A bluffside trail with an ocean view captivates a beginning hiker.

FEES

Day-use fees are now charged at many state park and US Forest Service trailheads. The fees and the location of fee sites are often in flux, so no fee specifics are mentioned with individual hikes. Bring a few dollars (or a pre-purchased pass) in case you are required to pay a fee at the trailhead.

SUGGESTIONS?

I've hiked all the trails in this book and checked road names and numbers and directions. But changes do occur; trails fall into disrepair; new roads are built or road numbers and names are changed; and old, abandoned trails are rehabilitated. I would appreciate hearing from readers about discrepancies in the hike descriptions and receiving suggestions of other trails that might deserve inclusion in the next edition of *Best Hikes with Kids: Oregon.* Please write to me in care of The Mountaineers Books, 1001 SW Klickitat Way, Suite 201, Seattle, WA 98134 or visit my website *www.besthikeswithkidsoregon.com.*

LEGEND

———	paved road or highway	～↯～	falls
··············	gravel road	❋ ❋ ❋	marsh
- - - - - -	trail	▬	lava
═══════	boardwalk	▲	summit
—·—·—·—·	wilderness or park boundary	♠	tree or forest
- - - - - -	ski lift	■	building
(5)	interstate highway	▣	point of interest
(30)	US highway	○	town or city
(138)	state highway	](	bridge
486	forest road	)(	pass
(T)	trailhead			gate
(L)	lookout	▲	campground
◗	body of water	⊼	picnic area
～～	river or creek	⪦	boat launch

Opposite: View from Spencer Butte

WILLAMETTE VALLEY

VIRGINIA LAKE

BEFORE YOU GO
For current conditions and more information, contact Oregon State Parks, (800) 551-6949, and ask about Wapato Access Greenway

ABOUT THE HIKE
Day hike
Easy for children
2.2-mile loop
Nearly level
High point 40 feet
Hikable year-round

GETTING THERE
- From downtown Portland, take US Highway 30 about 10 miles to the Sauvie Island Bridge
- Cross the bridge and drive north on Sauvie Island Road 2.5 miles
- The trailhead is signed "Wapato Access Greenway"; here there is parking for perhaps ten cars

HIKING THE TRAIL
Sauvie Island lies at the meeting of the Willamette and Columbia Rivers, northwest of Portland—a pastoral island of farms and fields, much

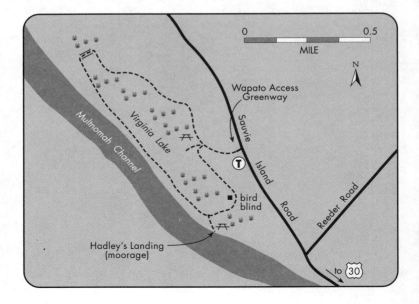

Virginia Lake

of it protected by the state as a wildlife refuge. The trail around Virginia Lake is a quiet beauty all year long. You may see birds on the lake; a blind helps you hide while you watch. You will see boats on the river where the trail cuts back toward Multnomah Channel. Bring a picnic and, in July and August, containers for the blackberries you'll pick.

Walk around the gate and down the trail heading out from the parking area. At 0.2 mile you'll reach a rise to the covered picnic shelter. For a clockwise hike, bear left, past the shelter, and drop down toward the lake, passing a spur trail leading directly to the lake (or, in summer, the marsh). About 0.3 mile from the start of the loop you'll reach a wooden bird blind. Cross the end of the lake and bear right at the junction, or detour left a short distance to Hadley's Landing, where boaters can tie up and hikers can sight-see or picnic with a water view. Continuing on the loop, the trail veers away from the lake's edge, following close to Multnomah Channel with frequent views of the water. Emerging from the trees, the trail crosses the north end of the lake at 1.2 miles and ascends a short rise, offering views of neighboring farms. The trail returns you to the picnic shelter at 1.8 miles; return to the trailhead as you came.

OAK ISLAND

BEFORE YOU GO
For current conditions or more information, contact Sauvie Island Wildlife Area, *www.dfw.state.or.us* or (503) 621-3488

ABOUT THE HIKE
Day hike
Easy for children
3-mile loop
Nearly level
High point 20 feet
Hikable Mid-April through September

GETTING THERE
- From downtown Portland, take US Highway 30 about 10 miles to the Sauvie Island Bridge

- Cross the bridge and head north on Sauvie Island Road for 1.8 miles
- Turn right on Reeder Road and go 1.3 miles
- Turn left onto Oak Island Road and drive 4 miles up and over the dike
- Trailhead is at gate at road's end

HIKING THE TRAIL
At the heart of Sauvie Island lies Sturgeon Lake, and jutting into the lake is a peninsula of tall oaks and open fields. An "island" on an island:

Sturgeon Lake from Oak Island

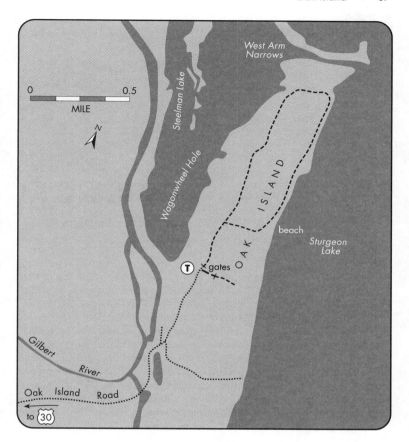

remote, breezy. There are views—sparkling lake through blackberry thicket—but it's the variety of sounds that strikes you here: the mixed chorus of birds, the wind in the oaks, now and then a jet approaching the Portland airport. The trail is closed to hikers during the winter hunting season.

From the gate, walk straight down the old road 0.3 mile to where the trail splits. For a clockwise hike, bear left onto the trail threading between oak forest and broad field, with the lake beyond. After rounding the end of the peninsula the trail runs closer to shore with good views of the lake, much wider on this side. At 2.25 miles, at a little pebble beach, a small hiker sign urges you to the right, back through the oak grove at the heart of the peninsula to the start of the loop. Follow the main trail back to your car.

TRYON CREEK

BEFORE YOU GO
For current conditions and more information, contact Tryon Creek State Natural Area, *www.oregonstateparks .org* or (503) 636-9886

ABOUT THE HIKE
Day hike
Easy for children
1.75- to 2.3-mile loops
125 feet elevation gain
High point 120 feet
Hikable year-round

GETTING THERE
- From southwest Portland, take I-5 to exit 297
- Follow Southwest Terwilliger Boulevard south 2.8 miles to the park entrance on the right

HIKING THE TRAIL
Portlanders are fortunate to have a variety of woodsy hiking trails in and just beyond the city limits. Tryon Creek State Natural Area is a stellar example. Surrounded by suburban southwest Portland, the park's 635 acres are forested in Douglas fir, big-leaf maple, alder, and western red cedar. Footbridges of all description cross Tryon and its feeder creeks. The outstanding trillium bloom here peaks in late March most years.

Begin hiking at the park's Nature Center, which has park information and maps, interpretive exhibits, and a gift shop. Hikers can create loops of any length on the park's intricate network of hiking trails (8 miles) and horse trails (3.5 miles, hikers allowed, few horses). Trails are extremely well signed. Come prepared for mud in winter. Here are just two of many options for loop hikes in the park.

CEDAR TRAIL LOOP (2.3-MILE LOOP, 125 FEET ELEVATION GAIN)
From the Nature Center, walk south on Old Main Trail 0.25 mile, passing Big Fir Trail, then bear left on Red Fox Trail to drop down to Tryon Creek at Red Fox Bridge. Cross the bridge, go another 0.1 mile, and bear right onto Cedar Trail. Follow it 1.2 miles—past Hemlock Trail, over Bunk Bridge, all the way to High Bridge. Across High Bridge, make a sharp right onto Middle Creek Trail, then bear left on Maple Ridge Trail to return to the Nature Center.

LEWIS AND CLARK TRAIL LOOP (1.75-MILE LOOP, 125 FEET ELEVATION GAIN)
This trail reportedly has the best show of trilliums in early spring and includes a trip across a bouncy suspension footbridge. From the Nature

Center, head north on Maple Ridge and Middle Creek Trails 0.4 mile to High Bridge. Don't cross; continue straight on the trail closest to the creek. In about 0.25 mile you'll reach Terry Riley Suspension Bridge spanning a gully. Bear right at the end of the bridge to get on Lewis and Clark Trail; keep your eyes open for the delicate white or pink flower. About 0.4 mile from the bridge, turn right, then a quick left to take

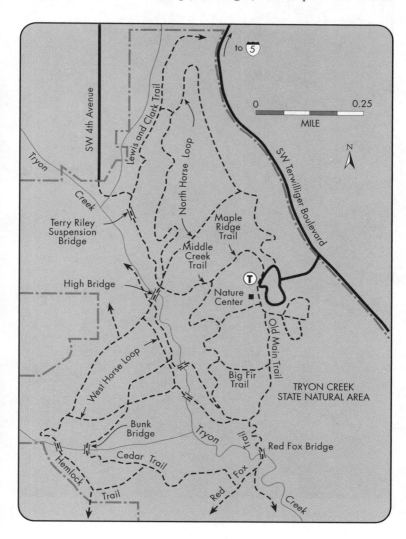

Footbridge at Tryon Creek

North Horse Loop 0.8 mile to the equestrian area just north of the Nature Center.

URBAN FORESTS: FOR A QUICK GETAWAY

In addition to the close-in hikes described individually in this book, there are lots of opportunities for forest hikes just outside and even inside the city limits of many Oregon cities and towns, from Astoria to Ashland to Bend. They're a great choice in winter, when the weather is iffy and you don't want to risk a long drive only to get rained out. In Portland, consider a hike in Hoyt Arboretum (twenty-one trails, 12 miles of trail, 8,000 identified plant specimens), the Audubon Society of Portland's Nature Sanctuary, adjacent Forest Park in the city's northwest corner, and Powell Butte in the southeast.

 SILVER FALLS

BEFORE YOU GO
For current conditions and more information, contact Silver Falls State Park, *www.oregonstateparks.org* or (503) 873-8681

ABOUT THE HIKE
Day hike
Moderate to challenging for children
2.3- to 3-mile loops
380 to 960 feet elevation gain
High point 1490 feet
Hikable year-round

GETTING THERE
- From Salem, take I-5 to exit 253
- Follow State Highway 22 southeast 5 miles to State Highway 214
- Drive east 16.5 miles, following signs to Silver Falls
- Turn left into South Falls Day-Use Area
- Follow signs to Picnic Area C and park at the far end of the lot
- The North Falls area parking is another 2.3 miles east and north on State 214 through the park

HIKING THE TRAIL
Silver Falls State Park is one of Oregon's premier family parks, with hiking trails, paved bicycle paths, equestrian trails, and a great campground,

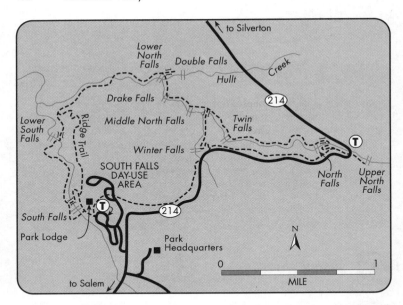

all in a magnificent forested canyon with ten major waterfalls—and less than a half-hour from I-5. Hikes here never seem long—surprises wait around the corner—but there's no denying the long climb back from the canyon floor. The park is appealing in all seasons, even winter, when sub-freezing temperatures nearly freeze the falls in place. But mist from the falls coats the trails with ice, too, so tour the frozen waterfalls with great care. No dogs are allowed (except on Ridge Trail).

The configuration of trails offers numerous options, from short falls-viewing jaunts to longer loops. You can see all ten falls in a 7-mile loop starting at South Falls or the quieter North Falls area. Here are three kid-friendly, short loop options showcasing two, six, and three water-falls, respectively.

SOUTH FALLS–RIDGE TRAIL LOOP (2.3-MILE LOOP; 440 FEET ELEVATION GAIN)

Follow the paved path past the rest rooms a short distance to a low stone wall overlooking South Falls. From the viewpoint overlooking 177-foot South Falls, follow signs to the paved path leading to the base of the falls. Turn left at the junction to walk behind the falls. Follow the path down to the footbridge at the base of the falls. Cross it for a short loop back to the parking lot; otherwise, continue down the creek's west bank on the now unpaved (and often rocky and muddy) trail. In 0.7 mile you will see 93-foot Lower South Falls just before the trail plunges down

187 steps and winds behind the falls. Continue 0.3 mile to a junction; bear right to take the 1-mile Ridge Trail up and out of the canyon and back to your car.

SOUTH FALLS–WINTER FALLS LOOP (3-MILE LOOP; 960 FEET ELEVATION GAIN)

Begin as for the shorter loop, above. At the junction with the Ridge Trail, however, continue on the main trail. Just past Lower North Falls, take the short spur up Hullt Creek to see tall, skinny Double Falls. At Middle North Falls, a spur leads behind the falls, but it's narrow, rough, very slick, and best avoided with kids. To complete the loop, turn right over the footbridge 0.2 mile past Middle North Falls and follow a dainty side creek to the base of Winter Falls. Continue to the top of the falls, emerging at a small highway turnout. The trail resumes on the far side of the turnout, staying parallel to the road for about 0.5 mile (and converging briefly with a bicycle path a couple of times) before heading off into lovely old-growth forest. When the trail meets the road, cross the road, pick up the trail again, and continue a short distance to a parking lot. Cross it, then follow a paved service road to the park's lodge. Walk past the lodge, then past the rest rooms, and arrive back at the hike's start.

Lower South Falls, Silver Creek

NORTH FALLS–WINTER FALLS LOOP (3-MILE LOOP; 380 FEET ELEVATION GAIN)

From the parking area above North Falls, cross the arching footbridge, bear left where a spur splits off to the right back under the bridge, then bear right at the next fork. In a few minutes the trail reaches the top of North Falls. Continue along the railed, cliff-hugging trail, then down 78 steps and back behind the falls in a wide, deep, dry cave. The sound of the falls pounding the rocks below reverberates in the cave, sounding like a jumbo jet at take-off. Walk with care; seeping water makes the trail slick in places. Continue downstream about 1 mile to Twin Falls, passing a huge, split boulder resting in the creek. Past Twin Falls, turn left across the north fork on a footbridge and follow a side creek up to Winter Falls. At the top of the falls, the trail reaches a highway turnout; the trail resumes on the left, following close to the road 1 mile back to the arching footbridge at the hike's start. Return to your car, or walk under the footbridge (and road bridge) and take a side trail another 0.2 mile upstream to see Upper North Falls, then return as you came.

 MCDOWELL CREEK FALLS

BEFORE YOU GO
For current conditions and more information, contact Linn County Parks, (541) 967-3917

ABOUT THE HIKE
Day hike
Easy for children
1.6 miles round trip or 1.8-mile loop
200 feet elevation gain
High point 1000 feet
Hikable year-round

GETTING THERE
- From I-5, take exit 233 at Albany
- Follow US Highway 20 past Lebanon about 4 miles
- Turn left onto Fairview Road between mileposts 18 and 19
- In 1 mile veer left onto McDowell Creek Park Drive and follow it 7.7 miles to the park, on your right

HIKING THE TRAIL
If it weren't for Silver Falls State Park (Hike 4), 25 miles north as the crow flies, you'd know all about McDowell Creek Park and its dazzling waterfalls. This small county park and its cataract-filled canyon isn't nearly on the scale of the canyon at Silver Falls. But in less than 2 miles you can see three waterfalls, from 20 to 119 feet tall.

You can drive to within a few steps of two of the falls: 119-foot Royal Terrace Falls and 39-foot Majestic Falls. For an easy out-and-back hike, start at the lower parking area and follow the trail 0.2 mile to a junction and go left; from a footbridge you'll look up to Royal Terrace Falls. Follow the main trail another 0.3 mile to the road, cross it, and continue 0.3 more past Crystal Pool to the wooden stairs and viewing platform at Majestic Falls. Return as you came. A right turn back at the first junction leads up steep stone steps to the top of Royal Terrace Falls—not much of a view—and through the forest, then down

Boardwalk and trail below Majestic Falls

a narrow path (that splits, both forks leading to the road), and you follow the road back to hook up with the trail. You don't gain much in scenery, and with no road shoulder it's not a particularly safe option with young ones.

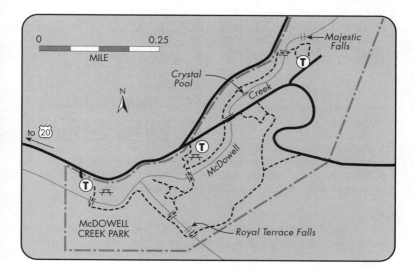

WHEN IS A FIR NOT A FIR?

Douglas fir, Oregon's official state tree, grows widely throughout western Oregon; you'll see it on most of the hikes in this book. The easiest way to identify it is by looking at the cones. They're 1.5 to 4.5 inches long, they hang down from the branches, and the bracts between the cone's scales look like  the hind legs and tail of a mouse trying to hide by scooting under the scales. Douglas firs are firs in name only; they are actually an entirely different species of conifer. Like all true fir cones, the cones of noble fir (such as those you can see at Marys Peak, Echo Basin, and Horsepasture Mountain, Hikes 6, 28, and 37) sit upright on the branch. They're big (4 to 6 inches long), with long, pointy bracts sticking out of the scales.

 MARYS PEAK

BEFORE YOU GO
For current conditions and more information, contact Waldport Ranger District, *www.fs.fed.us/r6/siuslaw* or (541) 563-3211

ABOUT THE HIKE
Day hike
Easy to moderate for children
1.4 miles round trip, 2- to 3.5-mile loops
337 to 660 feet elevation gain
High point 4097 feet
Hikable April through November

GETTING THERE
- From Corvallis, take US Highway 20 west through Philomath
- Turn south onto State Highway 34 and drive 10 miles to Marys Peak Road (FR 3010)
- Turn right and drive about 9 miles (becomes FR 3010 after a junction at 5.5 miles) to the gate at the summit parking lot

HIKING THE TRAIL
As the highest peak in the Coast Range, 4097-foot Marys Peak can feel like the top of the world. For a young child new to hiking, the 0.7-mile trek to the top of the peak is a great adventure, even if it is on a gravel

road. Older children may enjoy the longer, woodsier North Ridge Loop; all ages will enjoy the Meadowedge Trail Loop. Other hikes are also possible, including one-way hikes with a shuttle car (see map 6). Summer is the best season here, with penstemon, Columbia lilies, lupine, and other wildflowers festooning the upper slopes. Think of Marys Peak during shoulder seasons as well, when clouds sometimes swirl eerily among the noble firs and around the treeless summit.

SUMMIT HIKE (1.4 MILES ROUND TRIP; 337 FEET ELEVATION GAIN)

Walk the gravel road leading up (barred to all but utility vehicles servicing the transmission towers on the summit). The route is mostly above tree line, though you'll pass through stands of Douglas fir and noble fir. Be prepared for wind on top. A footpath separate from the road also leads to the summit.

MEADOWEDGE TRAIL LOOP (2-MILE LOOP; 480 FEET ELEVATION GAIN)

This trail was constructed with young hikers in mind. It passes in and out of woods and meadows, keeping things interesting and varied. From the gate at the main trailhead, take the summit road trail 0.2 mile to the signed start of Meadowedge Trail on the right. Walk the narrow path through the grassy meadow about 30 yards and enter a deep forest, where there is a trailhead sign and map. To walk the 1.6-mile loop clockwise, go straight at the first trail junction. For the

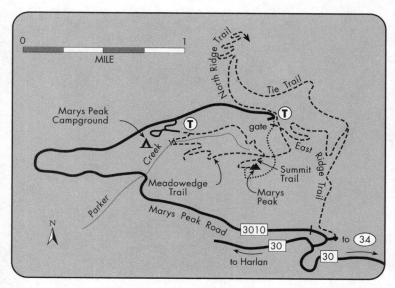

first few minutes you'll be walking just inside the forest's edge, until the trail enters a wildflower-strewn meadow. It loops back into the woods, which offer their own summer bouquet of bleeding hearts and oxalis. Wind down through the airy old-growth forest to a little bridge crossing Parker Creek, marking the loop's halfway point. Just beyond is the spur to Mary's Peak Campground, on the left. The main trail climbs just inside the forest until it completes the loop; bear left to return to the summit trail.

NORTH RIDGE LOOP (3.5 MILES, LOOP; 660 FEET ELEVATION GAIN)

The Tie Trail linking the East and North Ridge Trails creates a meditative, moderately graded, woodsy loop on Marys Peak. From the summit parking area, pick up the North Ridge Trail heading north, descending gently. After a couple of switchbacks, watch for a junction (easy to miss) with the Tie Trail, on the right at 0.7 mile. Follow it as it rolls along to the south to a more obvious junction with the East Ridge Trail at 1.8 miles. Bear right and climb the hillside switchbacks. At 3.1 miles the trail merges with a footpath leading down from the summit. Follow it back to the parking area.

 ## WOODPECKER LOOP

BEFORE YOU GO
For current conditions and more information, contact William L. Finley National Wildlife Refuge, www.fws.gov/willamettevalley /finley or (541) 757-7236

ABOUT THE HIKE
Day hike
Easy for children
1.2-mile loop
300 feet elevation gain
High point 420 feet
Hikable year-round

GETTING THERE
- From Corvallis, take US Highway 99W south 10 miles
- Turn west at the sign to Finley Refuge and drive 1.3 miles
- Turn south and drive 2.3 miles (passing rest rooms and an information kiosk at 0.8 mile)
- Park at the signed trailhead for Woodpecker Loop

HIKING THE TRAIL
Finley Refuge is one in a chain of three Willamette Valley refuges designated to provide winter habitat for Canada geese, including the

Opposite: Crossing Parker Creek, Meadowedge Trail

Viewing platform on Woodpecker Loop

dusky Canada goose, whose numbers have been dwindling. The best time to visit the refuge is October through March, when there are sure to be plenty of geese. This loop trail winds through a variety of habitats typical of this transition zone between the Coast Range and the Willamette Valley. It's the only trail in the refuge that's open through the winter; the others close to avoid disturbing the geese. Watch for poison oak.

Follow the trail past a signboard and a pond; look for frogs and newts. Just 0.1 mile from the trailhead, the trail splits to start the loop. Bearing right, the trail reaches a huge oak encircled by a wooden viewing platform at 0.3 mile; it looks out over a dry, grassy hillside scattered with more native oaks. Interpretive signs offer information about the area's ecology. From here, the nearly level trail winds mostly through a mixed forest of big-leaf maple, Douglas fir, and Oregon white oak, dipping also into ash swales and dense stands of second-growth Douglas fir. Five different kinds of woodpeckers have been identified in these woods. Can you see any?

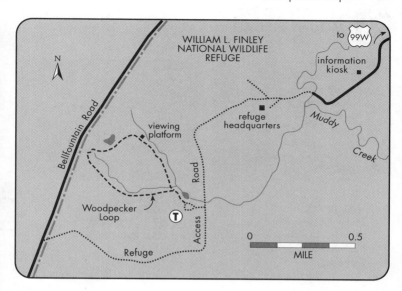

WILLIAM L. FINLEY
NATIONAL WILDLIFE
REFUGE

to 99W

information
kiosk

N

Bellfountain Road

viewing
platform

refuge
headquarters

Muddy Creek

Road

Woodpecker
Loop

T

Access

Refuge

0   0.5
MILE

LOOKING AND LISTENING FOR WOODPECKERS

Woodpecker Loop (Hike 7) boasts five different kinds of woodpeckers, but that's not unusual in the forests of Oregon. You might see them hopping up the trunk of a tree or flying between trees, or you might see the holes they've left where they bored for insects. Red-shafted flickers are the least flashy of the group; look for a pale spotted breast, a black striped back and a red "mustache." If you see a white head on a woodpecker in Eastern Oregon's pine forests, it's— yes—a white-headed woodpecker. Most impressive is the pileated woodpecker, as big as a crow with a flaming red crest. On Spencer Butte (Hike 9) and in other forests, listen for its call— a loud, insistent "kik-kik-kik" like something out of Jurassic Park—and look for its signature: big oblong or oval holes in trees.

MOUNT PISGAH

BEFORE YOU GO
For current conditions and more information, contact Lane County Parks, www.co.lane.or.us/parks or (541) 682-6940, or Mount Pisgah Arboretum, www.efn.org/~mtpisgah or (541) 747-3817

ABOUT THE HIKE
Day hike
Moderate to challenging for children
2.8 to 3 miles round trip
1046 feet elevation gain
High point 1516 feet
Hikable year-round

GETTING THERE
- From Eugene/Springfield, take I-5 to exit 189 (or take 30th Avenue South from Eugene)
- Cross to the freeway's east side and turn left, then immediately right
- Go 0.3 mile
- Turn left on Seavy Loop Road
- Drive 1.75 miles

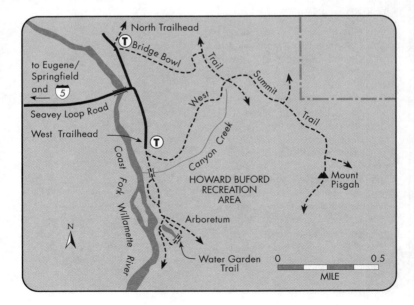

Sighting pedestal atop Mount Pisgah

■ After crossing the Coast Fork Willamette River, bear right to reach the west trailhead and main parking area, or bear left to reach the north trailhead

HIKING THE TRAIL

Above you, a red-tailed hawk rides an updraft, gliding out of sight behind the oak-mantled hill. Below, the silver ribbon of the Willamette River's Coast Fork unfurls along the mountain's base, bordering a patchwork of small farms: pumpkins, mint, you-cut flowers. There are many trails in Howard Buford Recreation Area, but for most visitors, including many families with children, the heart-pumping hike to the summit of Mount Pisgah is the number-one destination.

Most summit hikers take the West Summit Trail, which begins at the west trailhead, adjacent to the main parking area at the end of the road. Follow the wide, gravel trail through grassy meadows and in and out of oak groves. At 0.6 mile West Summit Trail reaches a junction with Bridge Bowl Trail—a good spot for a rest break. From here the trail steepens for a short distance, then moderates. At 1.4 miles it emerges from a grove of oaks onto the grassy, treeless summit. A bronze sighting pedestal, commissioned by the late writer Ken Kesey and his wife, Faye, is topped with a relief map of the surrounding territory; on the sides, bas-reliefs depict leaves and seeds, shells, animals, birds, fish, and other evidence of life forms that have dwelt in Oregon over the past 200 million years. Play I Spy—or bring paper and crayons or pastels to make rubbings. Return as you came. Alternately, start at the North Trailhead (see map 8) and begin your hike on the Bridge Bowl Trail—a slightly longer and less crowded route. In any case, while hiking on Mount Pisgah, stick to the wider main trails to avoid coming in contact with the ever-present poison oak.

Consider also the shorter, more level trails in Mount Pisgah Arboretum, at the mountain's base. Maps at the trailhead outline the many options such as the trail to the 1-mile round-trip riverside hike to the Water Garden, a good bet for spotting turtles.

 SPENCER BUTTE

BEFORE YOU GO
For current conditions and more information, contact Eugene Parks, Recreation and Cultural Services, *www.eugene-or.gov* or (541) 687-5333

ABOUT THE HIKE
Day hike
Moderate to challenging for children
3 miles round trip
770 feet elevation gain
High point 2052 feet
Hikable year-round

GETTING THERE
- From downtown Eugene, follow South Willamette Street south about 5 miles
- Turn left at the sign to Spencer Butte Park, on the east

side of the street about 1 mile before Willamette meets Fox Hollow Road

HIKING THE TRAIL
Forested Spencer Butte dominates Eugene's skyline, signaling the southern end of the Willamette Valley and the start of hilly southern Oregon. Like Mount Pisgah (Hike 8), it's a wonderful, close-in summit hike for kids willing to do some trudging for a top-of-the-world view.

There's plenty of poison oak and a car vandalism problem here as well. Unlike Mount Pisgah, you'll be hiking in deep forest with no big views until the big payoff at the summit.

From the top of the wide steps leading out of the parking area, go straight rather than left (left leads to a shorter—1 mile—but much steeper summit route), following the wide path slowly circling and ascending the butte. The trail can be muddy in the rainy season, though a boardwalk crosses the worst spots. At 0.5 mile go straight where a spur to the Ridgeline Trail enters from the right. Nearing the tree line, the trail degenerates into a tangle of trails. Do your best to stay on the main trail to avoid worsening the erosion here. If you're observant you can stay on some semblance of trail all the way to the summit outcrop; if not, you'll find yourself scrambling at the end. Note landmarks as you ascend to help you pick out the return route.

Once you've gotten to know the main trail up Spencer Butte, consider

Spencer Butte summit

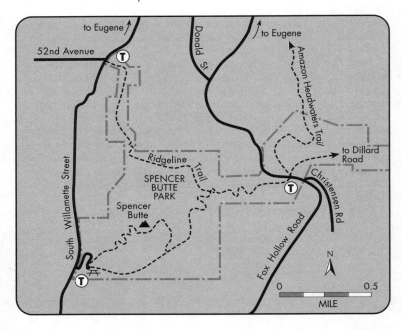

exploring the network of trails of which it's a part. The Ridgeline Trail offers almost 3 miles of hiking in and out of deeply forested ravines just below the butte. You can access it from several spots: a trailhead on South Willamette Street 0.75 mile north of the entrance to Spencer Butte Park, one 2 miles up Fox Hollow Road, or one at the summit of Dillard Road. There's a link to the Spencer Butte summit trail from the trail stretch between Willamette and Fox Hollow. The most recent addition to the trail system here is the Amazon Headwaters Trail, which spills 1 mile down the lush hillside from the Fox Hollow Road trailhead, crossing four footbridges, to end near the south end of Amazon Parkway across from Frank Kinney Park.

Opposite: Mount Hood

COLUMBIA GORGE AND MOUNT HOOD

LATOURELL FALLS

BEFORE YOU GO
For current conditions and more information, contact Guy W. Talbot State Park, *www.oregonstateparks.org* or (800) 551-6949

ABOUT THE HIKE
Day hike
Easy to moderate for children
1- to 2.2-mile loop
270 to 550 feet elevation gain
High point 700 feet
Hikable most of the year

GETTING THERE

- From Portland, take I-84 east to exit 28 (Bridal Veil)
- Drive a short distance to the Historic Columbia River Highway
- Turn right and drive 2.8 miles to the parking area at the base of the falls

HIKING THE TRAIL

As magical as most waterfall-blessed gorge trails are, this one seems even more like a path through a fairyland, especially in early spring, with butterflies dancing above pink bleeding hearts and white trilliums blooming

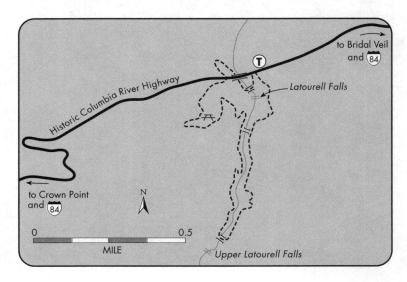

on the lush, green hillsides. Little footbridges and a huge natural amphitheater make the gorge at the falls' base particularly impressive. The trail is formed like a figure eight; for a shorter hike, follow just the lower loop. Hike it clockwise to save the best for last.

Left of 249-foot Latourell Falls, an asphalt path leads up the hill a short distance to a viewpoint. From here, the trail turns to dirt, leading to a second overlook near the top of the falls. Drop down (passing under a

Latourell Falls

tree overhanging the trail) to a footbridge not far above the falls. Stand on the bridge and close your eyes, not only to hear but also to feel the rumbling falls in your feet. If your party is game, backtrack a few steps to a trail junction, turn right, and follow the trail up along the east side of the creek about 0.5 mile to the footbridge at the base of Upper Latourell Falls, then continue down the west side of the creek to meet the lower trail just west of the lower falls footbridge.

From this middle bridge the trail drops down to the highway at a picnic area 0.2 mile west of the parking area. Rather than return on the road, cross it, drop down some steps and a couple of switchbacks, then bear right, following an asphalt path under the highway and over a footbridge at the base of the falls. Linger a while in this magnificent basalt amphitheater before continuing up to the parking area. Consider a stop at Vista House (see Hike 11) before heading home.

 BRIDAL VEIL FALLS

BEFORE YOU GO
For current conditions and more information, contact Bridal Veil State Park, www .oregonstateparks.org or (800) 551-6949

ABOUT THE HIKE
Day hike
Easy for children
0.7 mile round trip
150 feet elevation gain
High point 200 feet
Hikable most of the year

GETTING THERE
- From Portland take I-84 east to exit 28 (Bridal Veil)

- Drive a short distance to the Historic Columbia River Highway
- Turn right
- Drive about 1 mile
- Turn right into the parking area for Bridal Veil State Park

HIKING THE TRAIL
Bridal Veil Falls isn't more than 100 yards from the interstate freeway, but it's tucked around a corner so you can't see it as you pass in a car. For hikers, the roar of the freeway is drowned by the roar of the 130-foot, two-tier falls, sheeting over cliffs like a fine white veil. This very short hike, improved in 2005, is a good choice for very young children or as an add-on to fill out a day of hiking in the Columbia River Gorge. Lengthen it a bit with a walk on the park's paved interpretive trail.

To reach the falls, follow the paved trail northeast out of the parking lot, and at the Y, bear right. The paving soon gives way to gravel and starts switchbacking down the hill, crossing a short bridge in the process. Look for the mill pond and bits of a wooden log flume—remnants of the lumber mill that functioned here from the 1880s to 1937. At Bridal Veil Creek cross the gently arching wooden footbridge and follow steps back uphill a short distance to a viewing platform in front of the falls. Return as you came.

Back at the Y, a left turn leads onto a mostly flat, 0.5-mile paved interpretive trail along the bluffs overlooking the gorge. It circles a large field of camas, a tall blue wildflower that blooms mid-April to early May. Look also for wild lilies, iris, and lupine blooming here in spring as well. The path ends back at the parking area.

Extend your outing by driving 2.5 miles west on Historic Columbia River Highway to reach the Vista House at Crown Point, with perhaps the most dazzling views in the gorge. The octagonal, copper-domed Vista House opened in 1918. It closed in 2001 due to damage from almost a century of wind, rain, and snow. It was then exquisitely restored and reopened in 2006. Browse the gift shop and the interpretive displays, telling of the gorge's history and geology. It's open daily March through October. To return to Portland, wind west on the old highway another 4 miles to return to I-84 at exit 22.

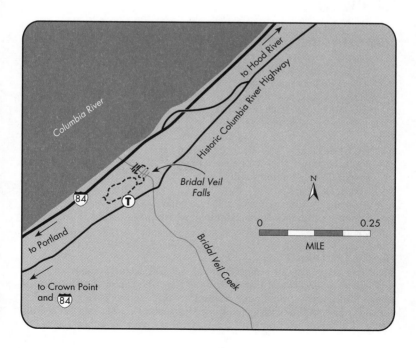

Columbia River from Bridal Veil interpretive trail

12 MULTNOMAH FALLS

BEFORE YOU GO
For current conditions and more information, contact Columbia River Gorge National Scenic Area, *www.fs.fed.us/r6 /Columbia* or (541) 308-1700

ABOUT THE HIKE
Day hike
Moderate for children
2.4 miles round trip
700 feet elevation gain
High point 900 feet
Hikable most of the year

GETTING THERE
■ From Portland, take I-84 east to exit 31 (Multnomah Falls) and park

■ Alternately, take exit 28 (or 35) and drive east (or west) on the Historic Columbia River Highway, which passes right in front of the falls

HIKING THE TRAIL
Most visitors to Oregon's most popular natural attraction don't wander any closer to 611-foot Multnomah Falls than the top of the stone steps above Multnomah Falls Lodge. Some take the asphalt path a short distance farther, to the bridge spanning Multnomah Creek below the falls. Fewer still follow that path all the way to the overlook at the top of the

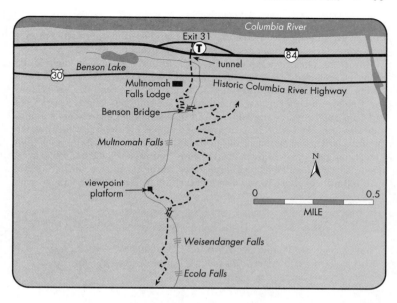

Beargrass

falls—a 1.2-mile uphill trek. For children, the hike to the top of the falls provides a sense of accomplishment and even identification with a prominent landmark that most people know only through postcards.

From the parking area off I-84, walk under the freeway, over Multnomah Creek and across the historic highway to reach Multnomah Falls Lodge. Follow the crowd up the path to the right of the falls, cross Benson Bridge, and continue up the trail. At 0.5 mile bear right at the trail junction and continue up, and up, and up as the trail switchbacks alongside the falls. At 1 mile a spur trail leads to an overlook platform above the falls, with a view not really of the falls but of the antlike people below. As long as your children aren't prone to unusually daredevilish acts, it's quite safe. Return as you came, or continue up the (rockier, rougher) trail 0.3 mile or more to see more waterfalls in Multnomah Creek.

A WATERFALL VOCABULARY

The Columbia Gorge has more waterfalls per square mile than anywhere else in Oregon, but there are plenty elsewhere as well. They come in many shapes and sizes:

Plunge: When the water free-falls from the edge of a cliff.
Horsetail: When water falls in one or more streams down a cliff face.
Fan: A horsetail that spreads out as it descends.
Cascade: Water tumbling over a series of rocks rather than straight down.
Block: A waterfall as wide, or nearly so, as it is tall.
Punchbowl: Where a narrow waterfall falls into a deep, wide pool.
Cataract: A very large waterfall.

HORSETAIL FALLS–ONEONTA FALLS

BEFORE YOU GO
For current conditions and more information, contact Columbia River Gorge National Scenic Area, *www.fs.fed.us/r6 /Columbia* or (541) 308-1700

ABOUT THE HIKE
Day hike
Easy for children
2.75-mile loop
500 feet elevation gain
High point 400 feet
Hikable most of the year

GETTING THERE
- From Portland take I-84 east to exit 35

- Head west 1.5 miles on the Historic Columbia River Highway
- Park in the lot across from 176-foot Horsetail Falls

HIKING THE TRAIL
This trail starts at a narrow cataract and heads up, offering something you don't get on every hike: the chance to walk behind a falls. The trail also leads you above and below Oneonta Gorge, a gorgeous chasm. Enjoy

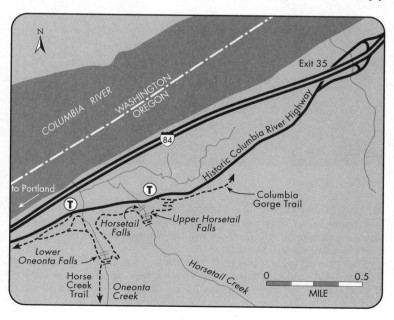

Horsetail Falls

wildflowers in spring, brilliant big-leaf maple in fall, and lush ferns in every season. Note that the loop hike ends with 0.5 mile along the road shoulder; take only children who will use appropriate caution here (or who are small enough to carry).

From the signed trailhead left of the falls, head uphill toward Upper Horsetail Falls (also called Ponytail Falls), passing through a garden of maidenhair and other ferns. At 0.25 mile turn west onto Columbia Gorge Trail and continue another 0.25 mile to the upper falls. (The hill drops away steeply here, but the trail is wide.) Here's where the trail leads behind the falls in a cavelike cleft in the basalt.

From the upper falls, the trail rolls along, offering views of the Columbia and the Washington side of the gorge. At about 0.8 mile the trail starts to drop and soon provides a view down into steep-walled Oneonta Gorge. Switchback down to a bridge crossing Oneonta Creek, listening for the roar of Lower Oneonta Falls below, then head back up briefly to a junction with Horse Creek Trail. Continue west on Columbia Gorge Trail. Proceed another 0.75 mile or so to the last trail junction, head down and east, and follow above the highway, dropping slowly to eventually meet it.

Finish the hike with a 0.5 mile trek back up the old highway to your car. **Caution:** the road shoulder is narrow in places, but cars on the old highway tend to poke along slowly. Be sure to pause at the mouth of Oneonta Gorge for a different perspective on the chasm already seen from above.

 WAHCLELLA FALLS

BEFORE YOU GO
For current conditions and more information, contact Columbia River Gorge National Scenic Area, www.fs.fed.us/r6 /Columbia or (541) 308-1700

ABOUT THE HIKE
Day hike
Easy for children
2 miles round trip
340 feet elevation gain
High point 380 feet
Hikable most of the year

GETTING THERE
- From Portland take I-84 east to exit 40 (Bonneville)
- Turn right
- Turn right again
- Follow signs a short distance to the trailhead at road's end

HIKING THE TRAIL
Waterfalls small and large, a gaping creek canyon and boulder garden, and bridges of various sizes all contribute to the charm of this hike, which ends at two-tier Wahclella Falls. Start hiking on a service road 0.25 mile to a diversion dam, which directs water from Tanner Creek to a downstream fish hatchery. At this point the trail narrows to a footpath along the canyon wall. A wooden footbridge hugs the canyon wall at a waterfall-washed cliff face; notice the basalt columns rising next to the trail. From here the trail starts a steady climb to a wooden staircase at

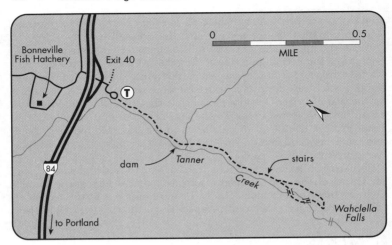

about 0.5 mile. Soon you'll reach a junction. The trail to the right leads to a bridge; cross it and follow the trail upstream across an old rockslide to reach the boisterous falls.

High water has washed the bridge out in the past. If that's the case, continue on the main trail as it climbs, and climbs some more, eventually dropping down to a bouldery falls viewpoint at 1 mile. The falls is a two-tier cataract, dropping perhaps 20 feet to a ledge, then bursting through a rock niche to drop another 60 feet or so into a wide pool. Return as you came, or loop back.

Extend your outing with a visit to the Bonneville Fish Hatchery, just across the freeway from the trailhead. Trout and sturgeon inhabit the display ponds year-round. There are always some fish in the hatchery raceways, too, but

Wahclella Falls

most of the action happens the last week in August through the end of November, when you can watch hatchery workers handling spawning Chinook and coho salmon.

 EAGLE CREEK

BEFORE YOU GO
For current conditions and more information, contact Columbia River Gorge National Scenic Area, *www.fs.fed.us/r6 /Columbia* or (541) 308-1700

ABOUT THE HIKE
Day hike
Moderate to challenging for children
4.2 to 6.6 miles round trip
Up to 480 feet elevation gain
High point 600 feet
Hikable most of the year

GETTING THERE
- From Portland take I-84 east to exit 41 (Eagle Creek)
- Follow the exit road to the fish hatchery
- Turn right and follow signs 0.5 mile to the trailhead at road's end

HIKING THE TRAIL
For squirrelly young children prone to bolt, you might pass on this one; it's a long, steep drop from the narrow and, in places, slick trail to the bottom of the canyon. For everyone else, Eagle Creek rocks. The grade is gentle, and it offers fine views of steep canyon walls, and even a water-fall or two. It's also one of the most popular and, hence, crowded trails in the gorge.

The trail begins as a wide, paved footpath (quickly turning to dirt) following Eagle Creek's east bank. The trail itself gains elevation faster

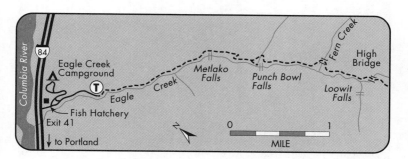

than the creek, however, gradually taking you higher in the basalt-walled canyon. After about 0.75 mile the trail narrows and grows rockier; a steel cable serves as a handrail for about 0.1 mile. Look for the large cave in the basalt cliff across the canyon.

PUNCH BOWL FALLS (4.2 MILES ROUND TRIP, 280 FEET ELEVATION GAIN)

After another railed, narrow stretch, the canyon and trail widen, with the creek out of sight far below. A signed spur trail leads to an overlook for Metlako Falls, about 0.25 mile upstream. At 1.8 miles a spur trail on the right leads to the base of Punch Bowl Falls. It's a steep, sometimes muddy, rocky, and narrow (not dangerously so) 0.2 mile down to the creek. With a drop of only 10 or 15 feet, the falls isn't dramatic, but it is lovely as it pours into a wide pool. The whole scene—a lushly vegetated

Gorge at High Bridge, Eagle Creek Trail

basalt grotto—is enchanting and very refreshing on a hot day. Back on the main trail, continue 0.3 mile to a view of the falls from above.

HIGH BRIDGE (6.6 MILES ROUND TRIP, 480 FEET ELEVATION GAIN)
For a longer hike, continue on the main trail another 0.5 mile to Fern Creek Bridge, a cool picnic spot, and 0.7 mile more to High Bridge. Here a footbridge crosses the narrow gorge, its creek inky black in shadows. Just downstream from High Bridge look for Loowit Falls, which cascades down a sheer rock face into a perfectly round pool, then fans down the cliff into Eagle Creek. Return as you came (though the trail continues into Hatfield Wilderness).

 CASCADE STREAMWATCH

BEFORE YOU GO
For current conditions and more information, contact Wildwood Recreation Site, (503) 622-3696, in summer; otherwise Zigzag Ranger District, *www.fs.fed.us/r6/mthood* or (503) 622-3191

ABOUT THE HIKE
Day hike
Easy for children
0.75- to 1.75-mile loops
Nearly level
High point 1200 feet
Hikable most of the year (road gated in winter)

GETTING THERE
- From Portland take I-84 to exit 16A (Gresham/Wood Village)
- Follow signs to US Highway 26 about 3 miles
- Turn left on Burnside Road (becomes US 26)
- Continue east on US 26 for about 28 miles
- In Welches, turn right at the sign to Wildwood Recreation Site
- Follow signs 1 mile to the trailhead

HIKING THE TRAIL
Art, science, and recreation all roll into one engaging experience on a pair of interpretive trails just off US Highway 26, on Mount Hood's west flank. The accessible trails lead through forest and marsh past a series of displays beautifully fusing poetry, sculpture, folklore, and biology to tell the story of the salmon's life cycle, habitat, and current prospects. The road from US 26 is gated from November through mid-May, but hikers may park at the gate and walk in.

Cascade Streamwatch Trail, a three-quarter-mile boardwalk loop just off the parking area, includes a spur to a covered fish-viewing

window set in a moving stream. Cross the Salmon River on an arching wooden footbridge to explore the 1-mile Wetlands Trail, with fingers of wooden boardwalk stretching into cattail marsh, beaver pond, and skunk cabbage bog. Oversized, weatherproof naturalists' "journals" provide arty, informative signage at viewing platforms. Follow signs to loop back to your starting point.

If that's not enough exercise, consider a strenuous 2.3-mile, 1400-foot climb to a view of Mount Hood and its forested foothills on Boulder Ridge Trail in the Salmon-Huckleberry Wilderness, which starts off the Wetlands Trail near the footbridge.

Artwork along Cascade Streamwatch Trail

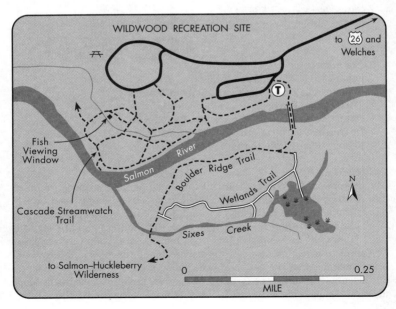

WATER: KEEPING IT CLEAN

Tempting as that clear mountain stream may be, there is really no place in the wilderness where you can be sure the water is free from *giardia*. This protozoan, carried by human and animal feces, can cause severe diarrhea of a type that can be hard to diagnose (but easy to treat once it is diagnosed). For short day hikes, drink only water out of water bottles filled at reliable sources—a home tap or a faucet at the trailhead. On longer outings, the simplest defense is to carry a portable water filter. Filters vary in cost and weight, but there are lightweight, reasonably priced models that can filter out *giardia* and other impurities. Alternatives include boiling water vigorously for one minute (three minutes above 6562 feet elevation) or treating water with iodine or other chemicals available at hiking stores.

 LOST CREEK

BEFORE YOU GO
For current conditions and more information, contact Zigzag Ranger District, *www .fs.fed.us/r6/mthood* or (503) 622-3191

ABOUT THE HIKE
Day hike
Easy for children
0.5 to 0.75 mile round trip
Level
High point 2600 feet
Hikable May through October

GETTING THERE
- From Portland take I-84 to exit 16A (Gresham/Wood Village)
- Follow signs to US Highway 26 south about 3 miles
- Turn left on Burnside Road (becomes US 26)
- Continue east on US 26 for about 29 miles to Zigzag
- Turn north (left) on East Lolo Pass Road
- Drive 4.2 miles to Road 1825
- Turn right and drive 2.4 miles
- Take the right fork
- Continue 0.3 mile
- Follow signs into Lost Creek Campground day-use area

HIKING THE TRAIL
A short walk on a flat creekside trail, with sunny decks over the creek to fish from or just relax on: You can't beat Lost Creek Trail for an outing with very young children, someone with impaired mobility, or anyone who

Lost Creek

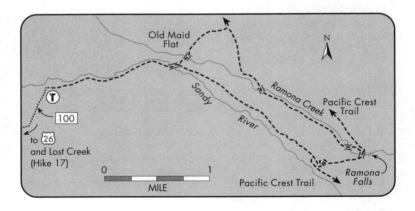

appreciates a gentle stroll through a beautiful forest. Like the Cascade Streamwatch trails (Hike 16), this one is paved for accessibility. Numerous interpretive signs add depth to the experience for adults and older children; little ones will enjoy the sights and sounds along this easy walk. The campground to which it is attached was built to accommodate disabled campers; it's quiet and shady, with lots of vault toilets. Enjoy great clear-day views of Mount Hood on the drive to the trailhead.

From the day-use parking area, start up the trail along the creek and follow it across a boardwalk to where it meets the loop trail. Bearing right along the creek, you'll pass several benches and will soon meet two spur trails, both to fishing and viewing platforms over the creek. The lefthand trail is longer, following a wooden boardwalk 150 yards through a salmonberry wetland. Back on the main trail, go just a little farther to meet another short spur trail to the beaver pond viewing area. The beaver is long gone, but the pond is inviting for toe-dipping on a hot day. From this point the main trail curves back to complete the circle.

 RAMONA FALLS

BEFORE YOU GO
For current conditions and more information, contact Zigzag Ranger District, *www.fs.fed.us/r6/mthood* or (503) 622-3191

ABOUT THE HIKE
Day hike
Challenging for children
6.9-mile loop
900 feet elevation gain
High point 3500 feet
Hikable May through October

GETTING THERE
- From Portland take I-84 to exit 16A (Gresham/Wood Village)
- Follow signs to US Highway 26 south about 3 miles
- Turn left on Burnside Road (becomes US 26)
- Continue east on US 26 for about 29 miles to Zigzag
- Turn north (left) on East Lolo Pass Road
- Drive 4.2 miles to Road 1825
- Turn right and drive 2.4 miles
- Take the left fork onto FR 100
- Continue 0.4 mile to a large gravel parking area

HIKING THE TRAIL
Ramona Falls is the most well-trammeled trail in the Mount Hood Wilderness. Children and adults like the variety the trail offers, including a memorable footbridge; a tall, lacy falls; and a mossy creek gurgling alongside the trail on the walk out. Consider hiking it in the morning, when the sun isn't yet too hot on Old Maid Flat. Following the loop route described here adds to the hike's interest.

The hike starts with a gentle ascent 1.25 miles to the start of Ramona Falls Trail at a tall footbridge over the Sandy River, milky gray with glacial silt. Immediately you'll reach a junction, the start of the loop route. Hike it counterclockwise to get to the falls a little quicker, albeit via a hotter, dustier route. The trail is fairly exposed for the first mile or so, with lodgepole pines lining the route, until it enters a cooler grove of Douglas fir. The river itself is rarely in sight but is within hearing distance most of the way.

At 2.8 miles you'll reach the junction with the Pacific Crest Trail (PCT); turn left and continue 0.5 mile to the falls. Standing in front of Ramona Falls on a hot summer's day is like standing in front of an open

Mount Hood from Sandy River bridge

refrigerator. The lacy veil of water playing down a face of worn columnar basalt is more like 500 miniwaterfalls, each sending cool air into the grotto at the falls' base. To preserve the vegetation around the falls, direct children away from the falls and to the creek below for water play.

The loop route continues past the falls (bear left where the PCT heads right) and down a cool vale following moss-banked Ramona Creek. About 1.5 miles from the falls, you're in hot lodgepole pine country again for most of the way back. About 1.7 miles beyond the falls, near a trail junction, keep a lookout for tree wells, formed about 200 years ago when lava flowed during an eruption of Mount Hood and swirled around standing trees. The wood eventually rotted out, leaving molds where the trees once stood.

At the junction, bear left. In another 0.6 mile, drop down, cross the creek, and arrive at the start of the loop again. Bear right to recross the Sandy River on the high bridge and follow the access trail 1.25 miles back to the parking area.

  SALMON RIVER

BEFORE YOU GO
For current conditions and more information, contact Zigzag Ranger District, *www.fs.fed.us/r6/mthood* or (503) 622-3191

ABOUT THE HIKE
Day hike or backpack
Easy to moderate for children
Up to 5.2 miles round trip
Up to 260 feet elevation gain
High point 1900 feet
Hikable most of the year

GETTING THERE
- From Portland take I-84 to exit 16A (Gresham/Wood Village)
- Follow signs to US Highway 26 south about 3 miles
- Turn left on Burnside Road (becomes US 26)
- Continue east on US 26 for about 29 miles to Zigzag
- Turn south (right) on Salmon River Road (FR 2618)
- Drive 2.8 miles to the lower trailhead
- Drive 2.3 miles farther to a bridge at the end of the Old Salmon River Trail and the beginning of the wilderness trail

HIKING THE TRAIL
Though it threads a narrow corridor between the road and river and isn't exactly remote, the Old Salmon River Trail has a particular charm for

families with children. It's wide and virtually level and offers a lot of river access. The huge trees of the old-growth forest it traverses are a big part of the trail's appeal. It's also accessible from many points along the road, so you can easily make short, one-way hikes with a second car, possibly a child's first backpack trip to one of several campsites along the trail. If you're after more of a hike, pick up the Salmon River Trail where the "old" trail ends and follow it into Salmon-Huckleberry Wilderness.

OLD SALMON RIVER TRAIL (2.6 MILES ONE WAY, 120 FEET ELEVATION GAIN)

Beginning at the trailhead closest to US 26, follow the trail upstream. There are huge, gorgeous Douglas firs and sword ferns alongside the trail, little footbridges to cross, and lacy cedars sweeping overhead. Bleeding hearts and oxalis carpet the forest floor. The Salmon River itself is particularly appealing on hot summer days, for anglers and others; it's deep green, alternating between deep pools and rocky riffles. Watch wading children carefully, as it is a river with a substantial current.

About a mile from the trailhead, bear right at an apparent fork (and at most other apparent forks; these are generally spurs leading back to the road). At 1.4 miles, the main trail itself leads out to the road at a

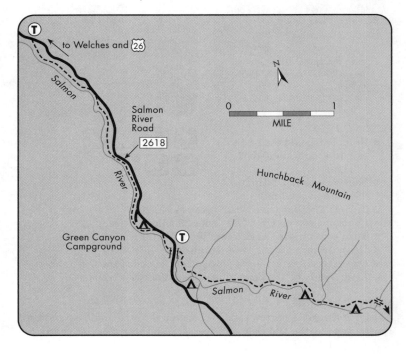

Old Salmon River Trail

point where the road is too close to the river to allow room for the trail. Walk along the road for 0.1 mile until the trail resumes and reenters the woods along the river. After walking through a portion of Green Canyon Campground, briefly wind up back along the road once more, 0.3 mile before the concrete bridge that signals the end of the lower trail stretch.

SALMON RIVER WILDERNESS HIKE (4.4 MILES ROUND TRIP, 260 FEET ELEVATION GAIN)

If you're seeking more challenge, pick up the trail at the bridge past Green Canyon Campground and head into the wilderness area. The trail immediately starts climbing, then drops to a bend in the river at 0.3 mile—a great picnic and exploring spot, and possibly swimming for the brave in midsummer. It continues to gradually ascend the deep forest, with huge trees at trailside. A good turnaround spot with kids is the side creek footbridge at 2.2 miles; beyond this point the trail moves away from the river. Back at 2 miles you'll find several campsites, but they're popular with backpackers in late spring and early summer and are first-come, first-served. If you do camp here, be especially careful about sanitation and use designated "toilet areas." The trail continues into the wilderness, linking with other trails in Salmon-Huckleberry Wilderness. Return as you came.

HIDDEN LAKE

BEFORE YOU GO
For current conditions and more information, contact Zigzag Ranger District, *www.fs.fed.us/r6/mthood* or (503) 622-3191

ABOUT THE HIKE
Day hike
Moderate to challenging for children
4 miles round trip
790 feet elevation gain
High point 3840 feet
Hikable May through October

GETTING THERE
- From Portland take I-84 to exit 16A (Gresham/Wood Village)
- Follow signs to US Highway 26 south about 3 miles
- Turn left on Burnside Road (becomes US 26)
- Continue east on US 26 for about 33 miles to just past milepost 48
- Turn north on Forest Road 2639 (Kiwanis Camp Road)
- Drive 2 miles
- Park at the trailhead sign in the large turnout on the left

HIKING THE TRAIL
The hike to Hidden Lake in Mount Hood Wilderness is a nice alternative to often-crowded Mirror Lake Trail (Hike 22). Not that they're really comparable; there's no view of Mount Hood from this lake, and it's a lot smaller and less accessible for wading. But it's quiet and peaceful and pretty—just what you need sometimes. As at Mirror Lake, hardy hikers can go farther—in this case, all the way to Timberline Trail. In late June or early July the rhododendrons lining the trail bloom with big pink blossoms. The moderate-to-challenging rating stems from the fairly uninteresting and, for the first mile, steep trail to get to the lake.

Hidden Lake

Start out climbing a series of switchbacks; pause at the fourth turn to catch your breath and admire the view of Laurel Hill and Tom Dick and Harry Mountain. Songbirds compete with the sound of eighteen-wheelers as you rise steadily and sometimes steeply for the first mile. Then the trail moderates to a rolling, gentle rise. The sounds of the highway drop away and you can enjoy the trailside rhodies and, in late summer, huckleberries. Nearing the lake the trail drops to cross the lake's outlet. Paths on either side of the creek lead to the lake and a pleasant clearing for picnicking (though too close for camping).

WHEN YOU'RE JUST TOO COLD

Hypothermia is a potentially life-threatening drop in core body temperature that most often occurs in cold, wet weather but can occur any time: on a windy spring day, for example, when you stop for lunch and don't bother putting a sweater on your sweat-cooled body. To help prevent hypothermia, wear clothing in layers—wool and polypropylene rather than all cotton—and peel them off or pile them back on as your body temperature fluctuates. Always carry (and wear, when necessary) good raingear. If someone in your party starts shivering; seems disoriented; has cold, clammy skin; or simply seems listless and whiny, get him moving, get clothes on him, and get hot liquids into him as quickly as possible. On cooler days it's nice to carry a thermos of hot chocolate or cider—or have one waiting back in the car.

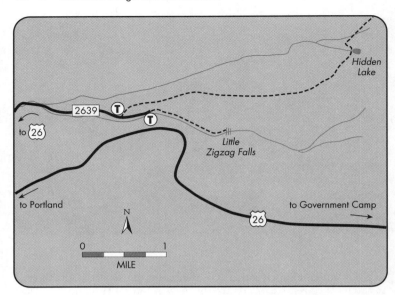

21 LITTLE ZIGZAG FALLS

BEFORE YOU GO
For current conditions and
more information, contact
Zigzag Ranger District, *www
.fs.fed.us/r6/mthood* or (503)
622-3191

ABOUT THE HIKE
Day hike
Easy for children
1 mile round trip
Nearly level
High point 3200 feet
Hikable April through
November

GETTING THERE
- From Portland take I-84 to
  exit 16A (Gresham/Wood
  Village)
- Follow signs to US Highway 26 south about 3 miles
- Turn left on Burnside Road (becomes US 26)
- Continue east on US 26 for about 33 miles to just past milepost 48
- Turn north on Forest Road 2639 (Kiwanis Camp Road)
- Drive 2.3 miles
- Park at the trailhead at the road's end

HIKING THE TRAIL

This is an ideal first hike for very young children on a visit to Mount Hood. It's just a few minutes' drive off US Highway 26, it's virtually level and not very long, and it ends at a lovely falls. Kids will enjoy wandering the easy path through the forest and playing by the pool at the base of the falls.

The well-constructed trail follows alongside icy, clear, swift Little Zigzag Creek through a lush, narrow canyon. Listen closely to the sounds the creek makes as it tumbles over rocks and logs and flows along sandy shallows; you can almost hear it converse with itself in different voices. Look for skunk cabbage in spring and blooming rhododendrons in early summer.

The base of Little Zigzag Falls is about 0.5 mile from the trailhead.

Little Zigzag Falls

Stand on the viewpoint—a structure built of rocks piled inside a cylinder of wire fencing—to watch the falls tumble about 75 feet in a series of short drops at the top, then one long cascade down an angled, mossy, chiseled rock face. The trail continues, making one switchback to climb to the top of the falls, where it ends. Return as you came.

MIRROR LAKE

BEFORE YOU GO
For current conditions and more information, contact Zigzag Ranger District, *www.fs.fed.us/r6/mthood* or (503) 622-3191

ABOUT THE HIKE
Day hike or backpack
Moderate for children
3.2 miles round trip
700 feet elevation gain
High point 4100 feet
Hikable May through October

GETTING THERE

- From Portland take I-84 to exit 16A (Gresham/Wood Village)
- Follow signs to US Highway 26 south about 3 miles
- Turn left on Burnside Road (becomes US 26)
- Continue east on US 26 for about 36 miles
- Park at the signed trailhead on the south side of the highway
- Westbound, trailhead is about 2 miles west of Government Camp

HIKING THE TRAIL

One hike to Mirror Lake, and you'll understand why it's so popular. It's relatively close to Portland and just the right length for a moderately easy hike, and the reward is a classic view of Mount Hood towering above Mirror Lake. Even on a weekday you probably won't be alone, so take particular care to have as little impact as possible by staying on the trail, keeping voices low at the lake, and scrupulously picking up after yourself. Consider hiking here in early summer, when the rhododendrons and bear grass are in bloom.

Cross Camp Creek on a footbridge and start up the trail through a Douglas fir, cedar, and pine forest for the first 0.5 mile, then cross a scree slope that seems to house a colony of little, furry pikas (listen for their call). Back in the woods, the trail starts switchbacking up toward the lake. The far-off sound of eighteen-wheelers grinding up the highway accompanies hikers most of the way along the trail, until the trail drops into the lake basin. Look for springboard cuts in tall stumps; a century ago, loggers cut down trees here using one big saw with a sawyer at either end. To get above the thick butt of the tree, they cut notches and wedged in a springboard to stand on as they sawed.

At 1.4 miles you'll meet the lake's gurgling outlet creek on the left and a trail junction, the start of a 0.4-mile loop trail around the lake. A sign indicates that campsites are to the right, and that's also the fastest route to the best lakeside picnic sites. The right fork arrives at the lake in just 0.1 mile. Rough stairs lead to nice picnic sites on this side of the lake.

Toward the far end of the lake, the trail splits. The left fork continues around the lake, granting postcard views of Mount Hood and following a log boardwalk across

Mirror Lake and Mount Hood

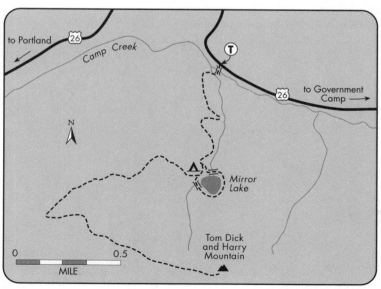

the lake's boggy inlet. The right fork leads steadily up another 1.6 miles (and 800 feet in elevation) to the top of Tom Dick and Harry Mountain, a worthwhile extension of the hike for older children after a pause at the lake. The trail here is less used and hence a bit rougher.

 TIMBERLINE TRAILS

BEFORE YOU GO
For current conditions and more information, contact Zigzag Ranger District, *www .fs.fed.us/r6/mthood* or (503) 622-3191

ABOUT THE HIKE
Day hike or backpack
Easy to moderate for children
1 to 4.4 miles round trip
100 to 500 feet elevation gain
High point 5900 feet
Hikable July through October

GETTING THERE
- From Portland take I-84 to exit 16A (Gresham/Wood Village)
- Follow signs to US Highway 26 south about 3 miles
- Turn left on Burnside Road (becomes US 26)
- Continue east on US 26 for about 39 miles, just past Government Camp
- Turn left at the sign to Timberline Lodge
- Drive 6 miles to the road's end

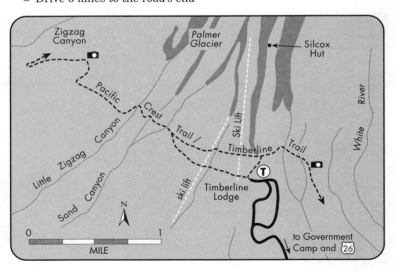

Timberline Lodge

HIKING THE TRAIL

A trip to grand Timberline Lodge, hand-built by artisans in the 1930s, is worthwhile any time of year. The round-the-mountain Timberline Trail (here part of the Pacific Crest Trail) passes right above the lodge, offering non-stop scenery and a taste of the alpine environment, bursting with wildflowers in midsummer.

WHITE RIVER CANYON OVERLOOK (1 MILE ROUND TRIP, 100 FEET ELEVATION GAIN)

For a short—but steep—walk, go east on the trail outside the lodge, heading up; it connects with the main Timberline Trail in about 0.25 mile, then reaches a view into White River Canyon at about 0.5 mile, at which point the trail starts a long descent. Return as you came.

ZIGZAG CANYON OVERLOOK (4.4 MILES ROUND TRIP, 500 FEET ELEVATION GAIN)

For a longer hike follow signs west from the lodge, ducking under a chairlift and into the trees. You'll pass through a succession of dazzling alpine meadows. At 1 mile, after connecting with the main Timberline Trail, the route dives down into rocky Little Zigzag Canyon (a possible turnaround point), climbs back out, descends through forest and meadow, then climbs to a grand view overlooking Zigzag Canyon and—on clear days—an array of peaks to the south. Return as you came.

Timberline's Magic Mile and Palmer chairlifts operate through Labor Day for skiers as well as visitors on foot (fee charged). Consider riding up and hiking the 2 miles back down, possibly with a side trip to Silcox Hut, just east of the top of the Magic Mile lift. The old mountain chalet—first the terminus for the original Magic Mile chairlift, later a rustic hut for climbers—has been restored and now offers lodging by reservation. Be sure to wander through Timberline Lodge, perusing the historical exhibits on the first floor. Just below the main lodge is the day lodge with a cafeteria and other services. Get prices and other details at *www.timberlinelodge.com.*

 UMBRELLA FALLS–SAHALIE FALLS

BEFORE YOU GO
For current conditions and more information, contact Hood River Ranger District, *www.fs.fed.us/r6/mthood* or (541) 352-6002

ABOUT THE HIKE
Day hike
Moderate for children
4.1-mile loop
800 feet elevation gain
High point 5240 feet
Hikable June through October

GETTING THERE

- From Government Camp, take US Highway 26 east about 3 miles
- Exit onto State Highway 35
- Take State Highway 35 about 7 miles
- Turn left at the sign to Hood River Meadows (Forest Road 3545), about a mile east of the turnoff to Mount Hood Meadows ski area
- Drive 0.4 mile
- Park at the signed trailhead

HIKING THE TRAIL

Summer hikes don't get much better than this. Early in the season the trail is lined with pale-green huckleberry leaves and white bear grass plumes; later the meadows are ablaze with wildflowers. Just about when the flower show starts to fade in late August and early September, the huckleberries ripen. Then there are the waterfalls and the views. The novelty of hiking across the ski runs at Mount Hood Meadows is fun for children who might ski or snowboard here in the winter. Although there are various ways to hike part or all of the trails around Hood River Meadows, this loop route makes a good, varied, moderate day hike for families.

For a clockwise loop, start hiking on the west side of the road, diving immediately into a field of huckleberries. The trail crosses a boggy area on a log, then leads to a creek that is crossed on rocks. Follow the creek up to a road, cross it, then continue up to Sahalie Falls, off the main trail to the left at 0.5 mile.

Back on the main trail, climb uphill steadily, following the East Fork

East Fork Hood River below Umbrella Falls

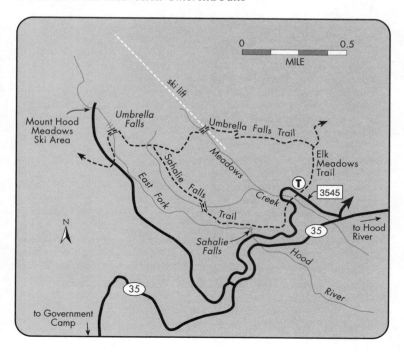

Hood River's east bank. At about 1 mile descend momentarily to cross a creek, then resume the climb, passing more little creeks and traversing some meadows. At 1.7 miles the trail reaches a T junction with Umbrella Falls Trail. Turn left and walk 0.3 mile to Umbrella Falls—a great picnic site—also on the East Fork Hood River. A bridge crosses the wide, sandy creek below the falls, which streams gently down a rounded rock face like rain down an umbrella. An asphalt path leads 0.2 mile to the top of the falls; continue a few steps farther to reach the lower end of the Mount Hood Meadows parking area.

To resume the hike from Umbrella Falls, return 0.3 mile to the junction and continue straight. About 0.2 mile from the junction the trail emerges from the forest and begins traversing a wide meadow (a ski run) with a great mountain view. The trail passes under a ski lift and continues in and out of forest and meadow for about a mile before re-entering the forest. After about 0.2 mile in the woods, bear right at the three-way junction with Elk Meadows Trail. Continue another 0.4 mile back to the trailhead.

FERNS, FERNS EVERYWHERE

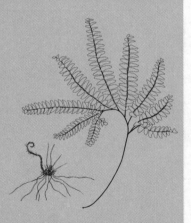

What's older than the trees in an old-growth forest? The fern family. As a family of plants, ferns are older than land animals and much older than the dinosaurs. They were thriving on earth 200 million years before the first flowering plants evolved. There are probably more ferns per square foot in the forests of the Pacific Northwest than anywhere else on earth— even the tropical rain forests. See how many different kinds you can identify on your next forest hike: sword ferns (the long leaves are shaped like the name), maidenhair (with black stems), deer ferns (slender and swordlike), licorice ferns (they grow only in winter, often on tree trunks and the crooks of branches), and triangle-shaped leaves of bracken fern, abundant in more open spots.

TAMAWANAS FALLS

BEFORE YOU GO
For current conditions and
more information, contact
Hood River Ranger District,
www.fs.fed.us/r6/mthood or
(541) 352-6002

ABOUT THE HIKE
Day hike
Moderate for children
4.2 miles round trip
360 feet elevation gain
High point 3400 feet
Hikable May through October

GETTING THERE
- From Hood River, take State Highway 35 south about 25 miles
- Pull over at the trailhead sign ("East Fork Trail") on highway's west side
- From Government Camp, take US Highway 26 east about 3 miles
- Exit onto State Highway 35
- Take State Highway 35 about 14 miles to the trailhead ("East Fork Trail"), just north of Sherwood Campground

HIKING THE TRAIL
Four wooden footbridges that surely shelter trolls, a waterfall over butterfly-shaped rocks, a steep talus slope: This trail packs a whole lot of interest per mile. All the trailside attractions (and the anticipation of more) help the miles speed by.

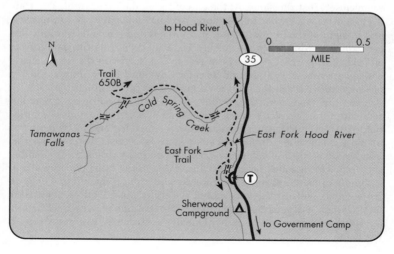

Tamawanas Falls

Walk through the campground toward East Fork Hood River, often milky with glacial silt, and cross it on a narrow log bridge. Two-tier railings make the bridge relatively safe for children, but you'll want to watch them closely just the same. At the end of the bridge, bear right. The trail leads north for a rather unappealing 0.6 mile, following above the river and in sight of the highway. After it bears left and meets a trail junction (go straight), things improve quickly. The trail drops into the cool canyon of Cold Spring Creek, crosses the creek, and heads up the noisy, moss-banked stream. Look at ground level for tiny bunchberry and twinflower blossoms or—later in the season—their berries (inedible).

Continue upstream on the rather rocky trail, rounding a big boulder at about 1.5 miles. Walk along the bottom of a scree slope past a junction with Trail 650B, then recross the creek on a log bridge. Switchback up a couple of times, drop down some steps, and cross the creek for the last time. This is a lovely spot—pool above, frothy drops below—and a good place for a snack before the final push to the falls. It's only about 0.25 mile up (and up) some switchbacks and around the hill to a view of Tamawanas Falls at the very end of the trail. The falls drop about 100 feet through a depression worn in a cliff of columnar basalt. Cliffs fan out like butterfly wings on either side of the stream of water. Return as you came.

LITTLE CRATER LAKE

BEFORE YOU GO
For current conditions and more information, contact Zigzag Ranger District, www.fs.fed.us/r6/mthood or (503) 622-3191

ABOUT THE HIKE
Day hike
Easy for children
0.4 to 1.2 miles round trip
Level
High point 3250 feet
Hikable May through October

GETTING THERE

- From Government Camp, take US Highway 26 east about 3 miles to junction with State Highway 35
- Continue south on US 26 about 9 more miles
- Turn right at the sign to Timothy Lake (Forest Road 42)
- Drive 4.2 miles
- Turn right at the sign to Little Crater Lake (Forest Road 58)
- Drive 2.3 miles
- Turn left into Little Crater Campground
- Follow the road around to the signed trailhead at the meadow's edge

HIKING THE TRAIL

Little it is: a jewel of a pond, its color an iridescent blue-green. The paved path to the lake is a favorite among the youngest and oldest members of our family. It leads through a moist meadow blooming all summer

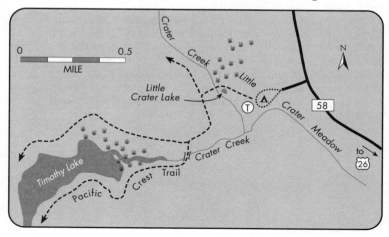

Little Crater Lake

with a succession of wildflowers—the tall stalks of white-blossomed hellebore held sway on our last visit. From Little Crater Lake it's just a few more minutes to Crater Creek, perfect for dipping toes on a hot day. At this point you're on the Pacific Crest Trail (PCT), with plenty of options to extend the day's hike.

Follow the paved path through the meadow, into a grove of trees, and to the wooden platform at the edge of Little Crater Lake. Signs explain how the lake came to be—nothing like the process that produced big Crater Lake. Rather, hundreds of years ago water was forced up through a crack in a fault line, creating an artesian spring, washing away the sandstone under the meadow, and creating a small but deep (45 feet at one point) lake.

Continue around the right side of the lake on the trail to hook up with the PCT in another 0.1 mile. Turn left (south) and continue 0.3 mile to another junction, the start of a loop trail around Timothy Lake. Bear left (staying on the PCT); immediately you'll come to a wooden bridge crossing shallow, 50-foot-wide Crater Creek. Its sandy bottom invites wading on hot days. Return as you came, or check a forest map to consider longer hike options, including a one-way hike with shuttle car to Oak Fork Campground (4.5 miles), the first of several campgrounds on the south shore of Timothy Lake.

Extend your outing with a visit to Clackamas Historical Ranger Station. It's about 5 miles down Forest Road 42 from the turnoff to Little Crater Lake. The 1930s ranger station alongside the Oak Grove Fork of the Clackamas River has been restored and is now period-furnished, from the potbelly stove to the photo of FDR over the desk. It now serves as a living museum and information center. Volunteer hosts are usually on hand in summer to share what they know about its history. It's a good spot for a picnic as well.

Opposite: Opal Creek

NORTHERN
CASCADES

27 OPAL CREEK

BEFORE YOU GO
For current conditions and more information, contact Detroit Ranger District, www.fs.fed.us /r6/willamette or (503) 854-3366, or Opal Creek Ancient Forest Center, *www.opalcreek .org* or (503) 892-2782

ABOUT THE HIKE
Day hike or backpack
Moderate to challenging for children
4 to 7 miles round trip
180 to 280 feet elevation gain
High point 2200 feet
Hikable most of the year

GETTING THERE

- From I-5 at Salem take exit 253
- Follow State Highway 22 east 23 miles
- 1 mile east of Mehama, turn left on Little North Fork Road
- Drive 21 miles (becomes Forest Road 2209); the last 5.5 miles are gravel
- Park where a gate blocks further access

HIKING THE TRAIL

After a long battle, in 1998 wilderness protection was granted to the renowned old-growth forest where Opal Creek joins Battle Ax Creek to form the Little North Fork Santiam River. Hiking here starts on a primitive

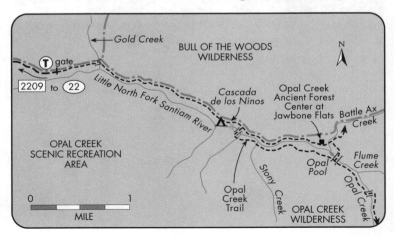

Old trucks at Jawbone Flats

dirt road leading to the old mining community of Jawbone Flats; the only vehicles allowed on this road are those used by the handful of residents of Jawbone Flats, now home to Opal Creek Ancient Forest Center. Some of the most magnificent groves are right along the road, with trees as much as 700 years old. If you don't get as far as the trails leading to Opal Pool and up Opal Creek, you can still have an awesome hike.

From the gate, the trail rolls gently through the forest, crossing Gold Creek on a 60-foot-tall bridge (be careful here). At 2 miles it reaches the former Merton sawmill site, which operated for just two years a half-century ago; look for a spur trail on the right leading a short distance to a view of 30-foot Cascada de los Ninos (waterfall of the children). Turn around here, or continue 0.2 mile more to the start of a trail, on your right, leading to an old log bridge across the Little North Fork. There's a little gravel river beach just downstream from the bridge—a good picnic spot and possible turnaround.

Continuing, bear left after crossing the bridge to follow the river to dazzling Opal Pool (3.5 miles total from the gate). You'll hear it before you see it: a roar of water charging through a narrow rock chasm before landing in a deep, clear-green pool. Return as you came, or extend your hike by just 0.25 or so by crossing the substantial footbridge just upstream of Opal Pool and following the trail about 0.5 through the forest and across Battle Ax Creek to Jawbone Flats, a circa-1929 mining camp that's been put to new use as an old-growth study center. Return via the road. Another alternative for day hikers is simply an out-and-back hike from the gate to Jawbone Flats (6.2 miles total).

WHAT IS AN OLD-GROWTH FOREST?

It's as hard to define as it is to define an old person—everyone has a different opinion. It's not just about the age of the trees, scientists say. Most agree that an old-growth forest is one that has had time to develop into a diverse place with both living and dead wood that supports a wide variety of plants and animals. Typically such a forest in western Oregon has a wide variety of sizes and species of trees, many of them 350 to 700 years old. They include dead and fallen trees that provide hiding places and nutrients to many other plants and animals. In undisturbed old-growth forests, old stumps and fallen trees known as "nurse logs" harbor new life as they decompose; you may see huckleberries and vine maples and even young conifers growing out of them.

28 ECHO BASIN

BEFORE YOU GO
For current conditions and more information, contact Detroit Ranger District, *www .fs.fed.us/r6/willamette* or (503) 854-3366

ABOUT THE HIKE
Day hike or backpack
Moderate for children
2.5 miles loop
640 feet elevation gain
High point 4800 feet
Hikable July through October

GETTING THERE
- From Sweet Home (southeast of Corvallis and Albany), drive about 38 miles east on US Highway 20
- From the US 20/State 126 junction, drive about 5 miles west
- Turn northeast onto Forest Road 055
- Drive 2 miles on a gravel road to the trailhead, on the right

HIKING THE TRAIL
The forest this loop trail traverses is probably unlike any other you've hiked through, with huge Alaska cedar, Pacific silver fir, and noble fir.

Echo Basin

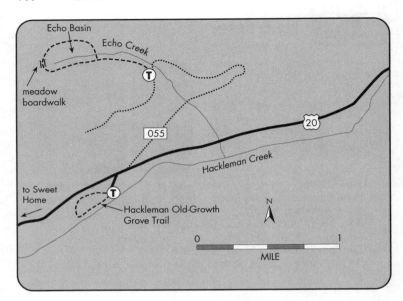

Not only is the mix of species unusual, but the trees themselves are full of character: many big, gnarly trees and stumps, some very old, some in strange shapes, some strangely tapered with huge bases and narrow, pointy tops. The hike includes a walk on a boardwalk crossing a bog full of flowers in summer.

The trail starts as a steady ascent, rough and rocky much of the way, with Echo Creek out of sight but in earshot. Stick with it for 0.6 mile to reach the beginning of the 1.3-mile loop trail through the basin. Go left; it's a gentler incline this way. Cross a few footbridges before emerging from the forest into an open meadow below high cliffs. Little rivulets cross the meadow, merging to become Echo Creek; fortunately the boardwalk across most of the meadow keeps you high and dry. Consider perching here for a picnic (mosquitoes might be bad early in the summer season). Continuing, the trail reenters the forest and descends, steeply in places, to the start of the loop and the route back down to the trailhead.

Round out a hiking trip to Echo Basin with a walk through Hackleman Old-Growth Grove, across the highway and slightly west of the start of Forest Road 055 (to Echo Basin). The main 1.25-mile loop trail is wide, graveled, and nearly level; a signed "primitive trail" offers a rougher, more adventurous (short) walk and better views of Hackleman Creek (but no real creek access). Lost Prairie Campground, about 2 miles east on US 20, has rest rooms and low-key camping.

IRON MOUNTAIN

BEFORE YOU GO
For current conditions and more information, contact Sweet Home Ranger District, *www.fs.fed.us/r6/willamette* or (541) 367-5168

ABOUT THE HIKE
Day hike
Challenging for children
3.6 miles round trip
1385 feet elevation gain
High point 5455 feet
Hikable July through October

GETTING THERE

- From Sweet Home (southeast of Corvallis and Albany), drive about 34 miles east on US Highway 20
- From the US 20/State 126 junction, drive about 9 miles west
- Turn south on Forest Road 15 at a small trailhead sign (milepost 63)
- Continue 0.2 mile to a large parking area

HIKING THE TRAIL

The trail up Iron Mountain is a pretty tough climb, but one tempered by the blaze of wildflowers that surrounds you at every step, and you're rewarded at the end by dazzling views of Cascade peaks. It's a favorite July wildflower trek among many Oregon hikers. No camping is allowed.

From the parking area, the trail cuts back through the woods, crosses the highway at 0.2 mile, and begins its climb with a gentle ascent through a deep, airy forest of old-growth Douglas fir. At about 0.8 mile the forest starts to open up, and at 1 mile the trail reaches a junction; bear right. In another 0.2 mile bear right again at the junction with Cone Peak Trail.

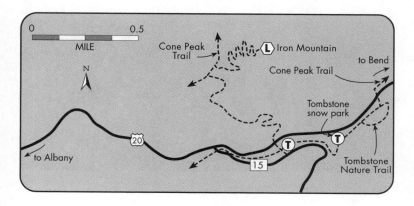

From the last junction, the trail is exposed (hot in summer) and quite steep. The consolation is the open fields of wildflowers blooming profusely in midsummer. Take time with children on this last 0.7 mile to the top, admiring the flowers and enjoying the view opening up as the trail ascends. The summit isn't much more than a rocky knob with a fire lookout tower; it's no longer staffed, however, and plans call to remove it and replace it with an informational kiosk. Watch children carefully up here; it's a long, steep drop from the rocky cliffs. Take in the view of Mount Hood, Mount Jefferson, Mount Washington, the Three Sisters, and the tiptop of Three-Fingered Jack. Return as you came.

This part of the Cascades is called Tombstone Pass. Find out why with a walk along 0.7-mile Tombstone Nature Trail after your ascent of Iron Mountain. Park at the Tombstone Snow-Park, off US 20 just 0.5 mile east of the turn-off to the Iron Mountain trailhead. Follow signs to the nature trail, which circles a lush meadow, and keep your eyes peeled for a replica of the tombstone for James McKnight, age 18, who accidentally killed himself with his own rifle in 1891; it's inscribed with a moving poem by his mother.

Mount Jefferson from Iron Mountain

TAMOLITCH POOL

BEFORE YOU GO
For current conditions and more information, contact McKenzie River Ranger District, *www.fs.fed.us/r6/willamette* or (541) 822-3381

ABOUT THE HIKE
Day hike
Moderate for children
4.6 miles round trip
200 feet elevation gain
High point 2400 feet
Hikable most of the year

GETTING THERE

- From Eugene/Springfield, take State Highway 126 east to McKenzie Bridge
- Continue east and north on State 126 about 15 miles
- Just past milepost 11, turn west onto Forest Road 730 at the sign to Trailbridge Reservoir
- Cross the river and bear right up gravel Forest Road 612
- Drive 0.5 mile to a bend in the road
- Park at the trailhead sign

HIKING THE TRAIL

The McKenzie River Trail offers a lot of opportunities for hikes, including one-way treks with a shuttle car. It runs 26.5 miles from McKenzie Bridge north to Fish Lake, with about ten access points along the way—and ten areas to choose from for day hikes. The 2.3-mile hike from Trailbridge Reservoir to Tamolitch Pool is one good choice. It's uncrowded and low enough in elevation to be accessible most of the year, and it follows close to the river most of the way. Although fairly uneventful, the walk to the pool ends with a view of deep, round, turquoise Tamolitch Pool, and a mystery: Where does the water come from? Keep reading.

The trail is fairly level for the first 1.5 miles or so. The McKenzie River is placid and within view much of the way. Cross a footbridge over a side creek after about 1 mile. About halfway to Tamolitch Pool the river picks up steam, tumbling and churning, as the trail gets a little steeper. You'll know you're getting close to Tamolitch Pool when a lot of old lava rock appears on either side of the trail, even underfoot. The trail stays above the river, granting occasional views down to the rushing water. Then, suddenly, the rushing stops, and you'll be looking down into clear Tamolitch Pool from atop a rock cliff. A sign calls it Tamolitch Falls, and it's easy to imagine the dramatic waterfall that would tumble down the sheer cliff at the far end of the pool if flows

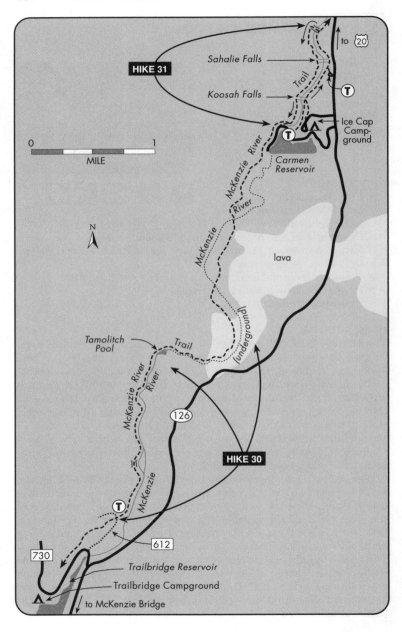

HIKE 31

Sahalie Falls

Koosah Falls

Trail

to 20

T

Ice Cap Campground

McKenzie River

Carmen Reservoir

T

0   1
MILE

McKenzie River

lava

N

(underground)

Tamolitch Pool

Trail

McKenzie River River

126

HIKE 30

McKenzie

T

612

730

Trailbridge Reservoir

Trailbridge Campground

to McKenzie Bridge

Tamolitch Pool

were high enough. Instead, the water seeps in invisibly. Above the pond, the river disappears into porous lava rock underground as far upstream as Carmen Reservoir. (Some flow would probably be seen on the surface if much of the river weren't also diverted from Carmen to Smith Reservoir, reentering the McKenzie below Tamolitch.) Explore, looking for tree molds left years ago when flowing lava surrounded standing trees. Return as you came.

With a shuttle car, Tamolitch Pool could serve as a stop on a one-way, downhill hike 5.2 miles from Carmen Reservoir to Trailbridge Reservoir.

31 SAHALIE FALLS–KOOSAH FALLS

BEFORE YOU GO
For current conditions and more information, contact McKenzie Ranger District, *www.fs.fed.us/r6/willamette* or (541) 822-3381

ABOUT THE HIKE
Day hike
Moderate for children
2.6-mile loop
400 feet elevation gain
High point 3000 feet
Hikable most of the year

GETTING THERE
- From Eugene/Springfield, take State Highway 126 east to McKenzie Bridge
- Continue east and north on State 126 about 22 miles
- Turn west into the parking area at Sahalie Falls (between mileposts 5 and 6)

HIKING THE TRAIL

Koosah Falls and, especially, Sahalie Falls are popular stopping points along the McKenzie River Highway. Trails on either side of the rushing river enable hikers to make a 2.6-mile loop that takes in both falls from both sides. The forest is lush, with tall trees, and the terrain is gentle. Kids will enjoy getting to see the two dramatic falls twice, plus crossing the McKenzie River on a high, narrow, log footbridge.

You can start the hike at several points; the simplest is the Sahalie Falls viewpoint. To hike counterclockwise, walk upriver (north), pausing to admire the falls from developed viewpoints along the way. Continue along the path 0.4 mile to its junction with the McKenzie River Trail. A right turn leads toward State 126 and Clear Lake; instead, turn left to cross a narrow footbridge over the river.

The trail rolls downstream through old-growth trees and past a small outcrop of lava, leading back past 68-foot Sahalie Falls, the foam at its base turning turquoise in sunlight. Continue down the trail, passing thundering 82-foot Koosah Falls about 0.5 mile past Sahalie. At about 1.7 miles bear left at a trail junction, leaving the McKenzie River Trail on a short spur leading to Carmen Reservoir.

The trail ends at the road around the reservoir. Follow the road to the left, across the McKenzie, then immediately look for a trail heading up the other side of the river. The trail up the east bank follows the river more closely. About 0.2 mile from the reservoir, pass a spur trail to Ice Cap Campground, then in another 0.2 mile arrive at a viewpoint overlooking Koosah Falls. Look for the springs gushing out of rocks at the base of the falls. The trail continues as a path and occasional stairs until it merges with the viewpoint trails at Sahalie Falls.

AN HOUR A DAY

If current trends continue, kids today face a shorter average lifespan than their parents due to the rise in obesity. To fight that trend, the National Institutes of Health recommend kids get at least 60 minutes of moderate physical activity on most, if not all, days. What else do they recommend?

- Drink water or low (or no) fat milk instead of sodas
- Fill up on fruits and vegetables
- Pass on high-fat, nutrient-poor foods like French fries, bacon, and doughnuts
- Don't spend more than two hours a day on "recreational screen time"—TV, video, or computer games

---

Opposite: Koosah Falls

CLEAR LAKE

BEFORE YOU GO
For current conditions and more information, contact McKenzie Ranger District, *www.fs.fed.us/r6/willamette* or (541) 822-3381

ABOUT THE HIKE
Day hike
Moderate for children
5-mile loop
Nearly level
High point 3040 feet
Hikable most of the year

GETTING THERE

- From Eugene/Springfield, take State Highway 126 east to McKenzie Bridge
- Continue east and north on State 126 about 23 miles
- Turn east at the sign to Coldwater Cove Campground (between mileposts 4 and 5)
- Follow the road to the boat ramp at the end of the campground

HIKING THE TRAIL

Clear Lake is an easily accessible and exquisitely pure lake high in the mountains. The level trail that encircles the lake is constantly changing; it passes through magnificent old-growth forest, winds along the sunny

Clear Lake

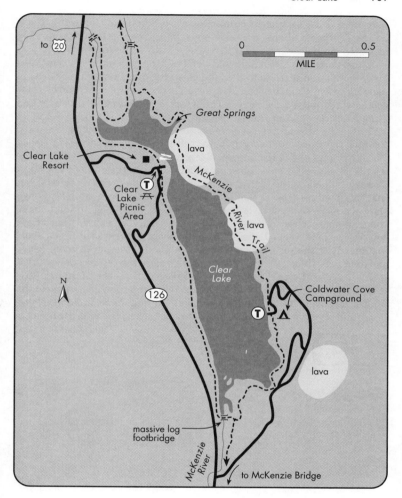

lakeshore, fords the McKenzie River on a log footbridge, and crosses over an extensive lava flow. On the lake's east side, the hike follows a portion of the McKenzie River Trail. Along the lakeshore the route passes a campground and a picnic area as well as a rustic resort that rents rowboats by the hour. No motorboats are allowed on Clear Lake, thus preserving its purity and tranquility for hikers and boaters alike. Wear sturdy boots; ankle-twisting lava rocks are sharp through thin soles. You could start the hike at the resort and picnic area on the northwest lakeshore. But starting a counterclockwise hike from Coldwater Cove, on the southeast shore, gets kids onto the intriguing lava flow quickly and gets the hottest part of the hike over with while they're fresh.

Head north on the McKenzie River Trail through big trees, passing a lot of anglers' spur trails to the lake. Soon the dirt-surface trail turns to asphalt when it reaches the lava flow. The vine maple here turns color sooner than in the forest, due to the stress of living with little water and among hot rocks. Continue across the lava for about 0.4 mile.

Enter the forest, then reemerge onto another 0.4-mile-wide lava flow. Reenter the woods and shortly pass a clear, blue-green cove—the site of Great Springs, one of the largest of several springs that feed Clear Lake. At 1.8 miles cross a streambed on a footbridge. At the end of the bridge, at a trail junction, the McKenzie River Trail heads to the right; bear left instead, heading around the north end of the lake. At a trailside bench there's a good view south to the Three Sisters. Following an inlet creek, the trail approaches the highway, then crosses the creek and heads back toward the lake. Clear Lake Resort is at about 3 miles; continue a short distance past the resort cabins and store and up the paved road. Leave the road near the picnic area's rest rooms, where the trail resumes. Cross a small, musical creek, then cross the lake's outlet—the McKenzie River—on a massive footbridge at 4.1 miles. In 0.1 mile you'll again meet the McKenzie River Trail; follow it to the left 0.8 mile more, along the lakeshore and across a lava flow, to find yourself back at the parking area.

 PROXY FALLS

BEFORE YOU GO
For current conditions and more information, contact McKenzie Ranger District, *www.fs.fed.us/r6/willamette* or (541) 822-3381

ABOUT THE HIKE
Day hike
Easy for children
1.25-mile loop
Level after slight ascent
High point 3200 feet
Hikable July through October

GETTING THERE
- From State Highway 126 east of McKenzie Bridge, turn right on State Highway 242 (east of milepost 54)
- Drive 9 miles to the trailhead

HIKING THE TRAIL
For a short hike to two spectacular waterfalls, choose this trail. Shortly after the highway leading to this trailhead opens for the summer

(usually late June), the rhododendrons and bear grass start blooming along the trail. A hike to Proxy Falls is a great way to break up a drive between Eugene and Sisters. Trailhead rest rooms are on the north side of the highway; the loop trail starts on the south side.

Proxy Falls Trail

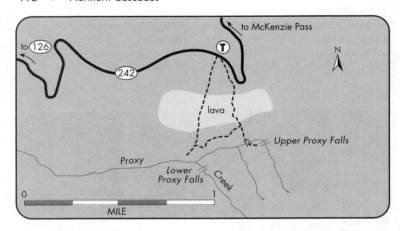

Walking counterclockwise, immediately head up, crossing an ancient lava flow. A spur to the right leads to Lower Proxy Falls, where Proxy Creek slides 200 feet down a curved cliff face, as if outlining a vase. In another 0.25 mile there's a second spur, to Upper Proxy Falls. Here water from springs high above fall more than 100 feet over a stairstep cliff thick with velvety moss. The placid pool at the base is inviting for toe dipping. Back on the main trail, continue 0.3 mile, crossing a little footbridge and that same lava flow, to return to the trailhead just east of where you started.

 LINTON LAKE

BEFORE YOU GO
For current conditions and more information, contact McKenzie Ranger District, *www.fs.fed.us/r6/willamette* or (541) 822-3381

ABOUT THE HIKE
Day hike or backpack
Moderate for children
3.8 miles round trip
300 feet elevation gain
High point 3550 feet
Hikable July through October

GETTING THERE
- From State Highway 126 east of McKenzie Bridge, turn right on State Highway 242 (east of milepost 54)
- Drive 10.5 miles to Alder Springs Campground (just east of milepost 66)
- Trailhead parking is on the left

Linton Lake

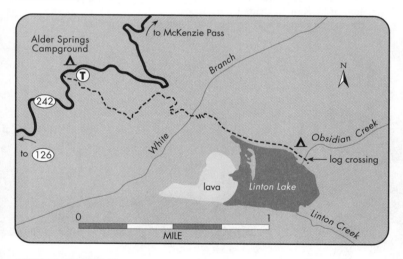

HIKING THE TRAIL

Trailhead parking for Linton Lake can be tight in midsummer—for good reason. It's a very gentle ascent to this stunning, deep green lake that feels more remote, more distant from civilization, than it is in miles. From the trailhead parking area, cross the road and start a slow descent through Douglas fir forest, climb a few switchbacks, cross a streambed, then drop over a vine maple-covered ridge at 1 mile. More switchbacks drop to where the trail levels and grants hikers their first view of the lake at 1.4 miles. Continue another 0.5 mile to where the trail dips to the lake near some campsites by Obsidian Creek. Cross the creek on a big log and follow an informal trail through the willows to a sandy beach jutting into the lake—a wonderfully serene, scenic spot. Return as you came.

BENSON AND HAND LAKES

BEFORE YOU GO
For current conditions and more information, contact McKenzie Ranger District, *www.fs.fed.us/r6/willamette* or (541) 822-3381

ABOUT THE HIKE
Day hike
Moderate for children
2.8 miles round trip
370 feet elevation gain
High point 5190 feet
Hikable July through October

GETTING THERE
■ From State Highway 126 east of McKenzie Bridge, turn right on State Highway 242 (east of milepost 54)

Hand Lake Shelter

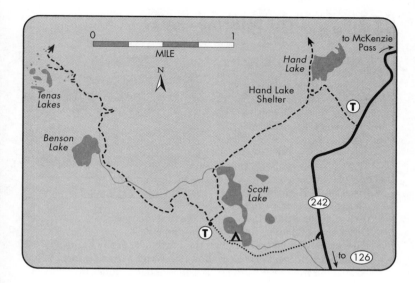

- Drive 16 miles to a left turn for Scott Lake
- Continue 1.5 miles on the gravel road along the lake, bearing left at the sign to Benson Trailhead
- Park at the road's end
- Trailhead for Hand Lake is on State 242, 1 mile past the turnoff to Scott Lake

HIKING THE TRAIL

Enjoy this gentle climb to Benson Lake through a subalpine forest to a high, cold lake. The trail climbs steadily, bordered by huckleberries and purple lousewort (a much prettier wildflower than the name implies) and shaded by alpine fir. There are no noteworthy landmarks until you catch a glimpse of the blue lake off to your left; an informal trail leads to a toe-dipping spot. Informal trails lead you partway around the lake in either direction. (The main trail continues, reaching a spur to the Tenas Lakes in another mile.) Return as you came.

Alternatively, or in addition, hike to Hand Lake, which sits in a broad meadow, golden in late summer. From the trailhead shared with Benson Lake, a trail leads past Scott Lake and through several meadows to reach Hand Lake Shelter in 1.5 miles. Bear left at the junction and continue 0.25 mile to reach the lake—not much more than a muddy handprint in late summer, bordered on the north by a lava flow. For a shorter hike (1 mile round trip) to Hand Lake Shelter, start at the Hand Lake Trailhead on State 242.

LITTLE BELKNAP CRATER

BEFORE YOU GO
For current conditions and
more information, contact
McKenzie Ranger District,
www.fs.fed.us/r6/willamette
or (541) 822-3381

ABOUT THE HIKE
Day hike
Challenging for children
5.2 miles round trip
1100 feet elevation gain
High point 6305 feet
Hikable July through October

GETTING THERE
- From State Highway 126
  east of McKenzie Bridge,
  turn right on State Highway 242 (east of milepost 54)
- Drive about 22 miles nearly to McKenzie Pass
- Park at the signed trailhead on the north side of the highway,
  about 0.5 mile west of rock-walled Dee Wright Observatory
- Westbound from Sisters, the trailhead is about 15 miles up State 242

HIKING THE TRAIL
It's a hike like no other, crossing a huge lava flow most of the way. Wear
boots; you'll shred your sneakers on the sharp rock. Is this a good kids'
hike? I wasn't sure until I asked a couple of kids, ages eight and ten,
halfway to the summit. Their response: all smiles, two thumbs up. "But
not a first hike," they cautioned, and their parents nodded. Later, on the

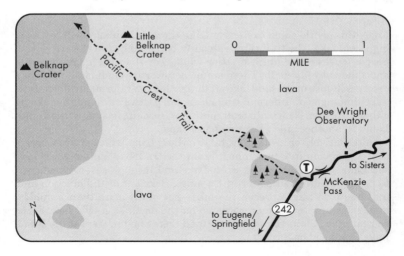

North and Middle Sister from Little Belknap Crater Trail

summit, I met three more children, ranging from six to twelve years old. Tough, but not too tough for motivated kids.

The route follows the Pacific Crest Trail north toward Mount Washington. It's not steep (except at the very end), but it's steadily up, with loose, rough lava stones underfoot most of the way. The trail begins in the forest, crosses a narrow band of lava, and returns to the trees for 0.3 mile more, following just inside the edge of a forested rise. (A lot of ripe huckleberries grow here in late summer.) At 0.75 mile the trail makes a sharp left turn and the real hike begins, with nothing but lava from here to the summit. At 2.3 miles turn right on the spur trail to the summit. The final few steps to the top begin with a walk and end with a scramble. From the summit, survey the gray-black sea of lava that surrounds your perch, with red Belknap Crater rising smoothly to the west and snowcapped North and Middle Sister to the south. Return as you came.

Extend your outing with a visit to Dee Wright Observatory, a rock parapet and viewpoint above the highway at McKenzie Pass. The paved Lava River Trail starts here and loops for 0.5 mile through the volcanic landscape.

THE PACIFIC CREST TRAIL: COULD YOU DO IT?

The Pacific Crest Trail is a 2650-mile hiking trail that starts at the border with Mexico, runs north through the deserts and high mountains of California and the Oregon and Washington Cascades and ends at the border with Canada. It is one of the world's longest continuous trails. Of the 300 or so people who attempt to hike it end-to-end—they're known as "through hikers"—each year, a little more than half finish it. Thousands more hikers follow stretches of it on day hikes or backpack trips. You may be one of them! Several hikes in this book follow or cross the PCT: Hikes 23 and 26 on Mount Hood and Hikes 36, 47, and 50 in the Cascades south of Mount Hood. To get to Canada before the autumn snowfall, through hikers have to walk at least 20 miles a day, carrying all their gear and several days' worth of food. Could you do it? Want to try someday?

 HORSEPASTURE MOUNTAIN

BEFORE YOU GO
For current conditions and more information, contact McKenzie Ranger District, *www.fs.fed.us/r6/willamette* or (541) 822-3381

ABOUT THE HIKE
Day hike
Moderate for children
2.8 miles round trip
910 feet elevation gain
High point 5660 feet
Hikable July through October

GETTING THERE
- From Eugene/Springfield, take State Highway 126 east 50 miles to McKenzie Bridge
- Turn right on Horse Creek Road
- Drive 2 miles to Forest Road 1993
- Turn right and continue 8.7 miles on the mostly paved, one-lane road
- Park along the road at the trailhead, on the right

HIKING THE TRAIL
Pick a clear day, preferably early in the summer season, for this hike. From the summit, the Three Sisters, Mount Washington, Mount Jefferson, and Bachelor Butte all seem so close you can almost touch them. If it's clear enough you may even see Mount Hood to the north and Diamond Peak to

the south. They're more stunning still with a mantle of snow. The wildflower show starts as soon as the snow melts and stays brilliant well into July.

Just 50 yards up the trail you'll reach a four-way junction; turn left and begin a steady climb through the forest, looking for ripe huckleberries in August. About halfway to the top the trail opens up to a mix of forest and alpine meadows. Finally the forest gives way to the mountain's bald top for the final 0.2 mile of switchbacks to the rocky summit, once the site of a fire lookout tower. Return, in no great rush, as you came.

Noble firs on Horsepasture Mountain

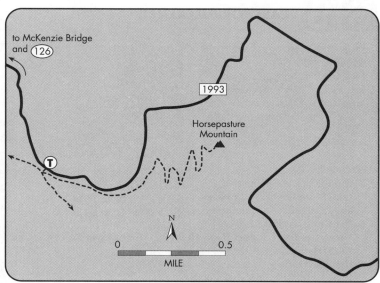

FAVORITE SUMMER WILDFLOWERS OF THE OREGON CASCADES

Paintbrush (at right): With its scarlet blossom, it looks just like a brush dipped in red paint; 6 to 18 inches tall.

Western pasque flower, or old man of the mountain: Starts out as a cream-colored buttercup about 5 inches tall; ends the season as a mophead of silky, greenish tassels nearly 2 feet tall.

Cat's ear, or mariposa lily: Inside the yellow cup formed by its three creamy petals are soft hairs; 3 to 8 inches tall.

Elephanthead: Tall flower stalks are covered with dozens of tiny purple blossoms that look like flaring elephant ears and trunks; 1 to 2 feet tall.

Columbine: The bright red, five-petal blossom nodding at the end of a slender stalk looks a little like an eagle's claw; 1.5 to 3 feet tall.

 EAST FORK MCKENZIE

BEFORE YOU GO
For current conditions and more information, contact McKenzie River Ranger District, *www.fs.fed.us/r6/willamette* or (541) 822-3381

ABOUT THE HIKE
Day hike
Easy to moderate for children
2.5 miles round trip
380 feet elevation gain
High point 2200 feet
Hikable most of the year

GETTING THERE
- From Eugene/Springfield, take State Highway 126 east about 40 miles to Blue River
- Continue on State 126 east about 4 miles to Forest Road 19 (at sign for Cougar Reservoir and Aufderheide Forest Drive)
- Drive 0.3 mile
- Bear right with Forest Road 19

- Continue another 2.9 miles
- Turn left across the dam onto Forest Road 1993
- Drive 2.5 miles to a three-way split in the road
- Take the middle road a short distance to trailhead parking

HIKING THE TRAIL

Not far from the better-known trail up French Pete Creek, the trail up the McKenzie River's East Fork doesn't look like much at the trailhead but unfolds into a lovely riverside walk through a mixed-age forest, with views of the mossy river—more like a boisterous creek—all the way.

The trail starts along a muddy, stump-filled arm of Cougar Reservoir in earshot of the road, but within minutes you're deep in the forest, and the creek is wild and free, tumbling icily over smooth river rocks. It's 0.25 mile to the first footbridge, a hand-planed log with railings on either side that takes you to the creek's south side, well beyond any traffic noise. Go another 0.25 mile to where a feeder creek in flood scoured a gully and even—look closely—tore the bark right off large trees on the uphill side, leaving a pile of logs and debris down in the main creek. Continue another 0.75 mile to the second bridge, a good turnaround spot. **Caution:** watch young children carefully, as there's

East Fork McKenzie River

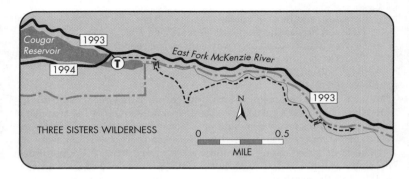

railing on only one side of the log bridge. Depending upon water level, you might be safe wading in the creek, which is easy to reach on foot here. Enjoy. Stretch your legs farther up the trail, heading deeper into Three Sisters Wilderness, or simply return as you came.

 FALL CREEK

BEFORE YOU GO
For current conditions and more information, contact Middle Fork Ranger District, *www.fs.fed.us/r6/willamette* or (541) 782-2283

ABOUT THE HIKE
Day hike
Easy to moderate for children
3.5 miles one way
120 feet elevation gain
High point 1000 feet
Hikable year-round

GETTING THERE
- From Eugene take I-5 south to State Highway 58
- Drive to the covered bridge at Lowell (just past milepost 13)

- Turn left and follow signs 3 miles north toward Fall Creek
- Turn right onto Fall Creek Road just before the Unity Covered Bridge
- Drive 10 miles (becomes Forest Road 18) to the lower trailhead on the right, across the road from Dolly Varden Campground
- Upper trailhead at Johnny Creek Nature Trail is about 3 miles up the road on the right

HIKING THE TRAIL
Long a favorite with local families, 14-mile Fall Creek Trail was devastated by a massive forest fire in 2003. Where tall trees once embraced

the bouldery creek, now blackened snags line the sun-washed trail and pink fireweed blossoms reach high along the trailside.

Fire spared the trail's lower stretch, however; it still has that deep forest magic. Hike it out and back from either end, or use a shuttle car for a one-way trek. From the lower trailhead, the trail rolls gently along Fall Creek, crossing a series of side creeks on footbridges, until you can spot the railings at Big Pool Campground, across the river, at 1.5 miles. More footbridges follow, and more opportunities to sneak down to the creekside for a picnic or a pause. At 3 miles the trail leads over a substantial log bridge crossing Timber Creek. It emerges near the end of an informal campground at the end of a gravel road just downstream from Johnny Creek Nature Trail. (To pick up the trail from this end, park at the nature trail just off Forest Road 18, and walk the short distance back to Forest Road 18, then pick up the gravel road on the south bank, watching for a more formal trail to emerge along the creek.)

The good news about the fire: with the tree canopy gone along much of the trail above Johnny Creek, the creekside boulders are bathed in sun all day, making the swimming holes along here even more appealing. The water is icy but clear. Consider a dip (supervised by adults) at Bedrock or Puma Creek Campgrounds or at less-crowded spots along the trail.

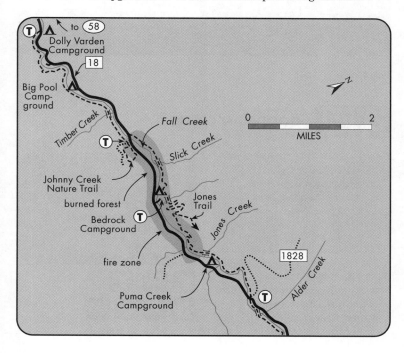

Fall Creek

 GOODMAN CREEK

BEFORE YOU GO
For current conditions and
more information, contact
Middle Fork Ranger District,
www.fs.fed.us/r6/willamette
or (541) 782-2283

ABOUT THE HIKE
Day hike or backpack
Moderate for children
4 miles round trip
300 feet elevation gain
High point 1150 feet
Hikable year-round

GETTING THERE
- From Eugene take I-5 south
  to State Highway 58
- Just west of milepost 21, pull
  off State 58 at wide trailhead parking area on right

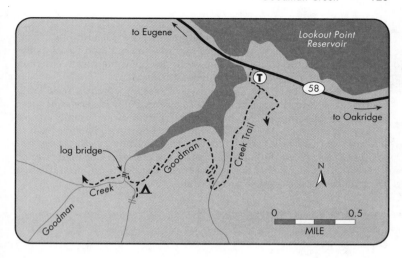

Goodman Creek

HIKING THE TRAIL

A gentle walk through stunning old-growth forest, leading to a foot-bridge across a lovely, wide stream: the hike to Goodman Creek is appealing year-round. In late winter you'll see plenty of newts crawling across the trail; later look for trilliums at trailside.

Just 0.2 mile from the trailhead you'll meet Goodman Creek Trail; bear right. The trail rounds an arm of Lookout Point Reservoir at some distance (a blessing, for it's not particularly scenic, especially at low winter water levels). At 1.9 miles there's a campsite and a spur leading left to a lovely waterfall and swimming hole. Continue on the main trail another 0.1 mile to the long log footbridge crossing Goodman Creek. This is a great picnic spot and a good turnaround with children (though the trail continues). Return as you came.

NEWTS: SAVED BY THEIR SKIN

The rough-skinned newt is a common sight on moist Cascades trails and at the edges of many lakes. But it can be hard to spot, given its coloring: muddy brown on top. It's the flash of orange belly that gives it away. There are many other salamander species in Oregon, but this one is most often out during the day because of the toxic skin secretions it has that protect it from predators. It's safe enough for humans to pick up and hold, but the poison it secretes is enough to sicken or kill a small animal that might eat it.

SPIRIT AND MOON FALLS

BEFORE YOU GO
For current conditions and more information, contact Cottage Grove Ranger District, www.fs.fed.us/r6/umpqua or (541) 767-5000

ABOUT THE HIKE
Day hike
Easy for children
0.8 or 1.2 miles round trip
100 to 200 feet elevation gain
High point 3100 feet
Hikable most of the year

GETTING THERE

- From Eugene take I-5 south to State Highway 58
- Just east of milepost 24, turn right off State 58 onto Patterson Mountain Road (Forest Road 5840)
- Bear right at the first Y
- Drive 9.7 miles up and over Patterson Saddle (becomes Forest Road 17)
- Turn left onto Forest Road 1790
- Trailhead for Spirit Falls is immediately on the right
- To Moon Falls, continue 0.2 mile
- Bear left on Forest Road 1702
- Drive 2.8 miles to Forest Road 1702-728
- Turn right and drive 0.3 mile to Forest Road 1702-203
- Bear left and continue 0.1 mile to the trailhead at road's end

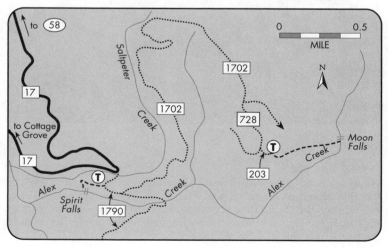

Spirit Falls

HIKING THE TRAIL

Hikes to either of these enchanting waterfalls are so short and so close together that you might as well visit both. The names are alluring enough, and they fulfill their promise of magic to hikers, especially those visiting in spring, when stream flows are high, or in summer, when cooling mists from the falls are most welcome.

SPIRIT FALLS (0.8 MILE ROUND TRIP, 200 FEET ELEVATION GAIN)
The trail drops gently, levels somewhat, and then begins to drop rather steeply down a dirt path that's slippery when wet. It ends at the base of 60-foot Spirit Falls, which gushes over domed cliffs. There's a picnic table at a viewpoint overlooking the falls, and the pool at the base of the um-brellalike falls is small and inviting for wading (though swimming, per se, is prohibited in the Layng Creek watershed). Return as you came.

MOON FALLS (1.2 MILES ROUND TRIP, 100 FEET ELEVATION GAIN)
Begin walking along the overgrown spur road you drove in on. At about 0.3 mile the route turns into a narrow forest footpath. As you hike in, listen for the low booming of grouse. The trail ends at the base of the falls, which streams down a broad cliff in rivulets that run together before plunging into the pool below. Plan to linger a while at the falls, watching for water ouzels dipping in the stream, exploring the pool and Alex Creek, and perhaps picnicking at a table there. Return as you came.

 BRICE CREEK

BEFORE YOU GO
For current conditions and more information, contact Cottage Grove Ranger District, *www.fs.fed.us/r6/umpqua* or (541) 767-5000

ABOUT THE HIKE
Day hike or backpack
Easy to challenging for children
2 miles or more round trip
Up to 900 feet elevation gain
High point 2800 feet
Hikable most of the year

GETTING THERE
- From I-5 at Cottage Grove (exit 174), follow signs to Row River Road
- Stay on the main road toward Dorena Reservoir for 19.5 miles, passing through the hamlets of Dorena and Culp Creek and bearing right at junction with Lower Brice Creek Road
- Bear right at the Y onto Brice Creek Road
- Drive 3 miles to the West End Trailhead (parking on right)
- Continue to trailheads at Cedar Creek, Lund Park, or Champion Creek (also known as East End)

HIKING THE TRAIL
With its bedrock pools and falls enticing swimmers, and the huge Douglas firs and cedars lining its banks, Brice Creek is exceptional. A little-used

road follows the river on the opposite bank, making it a less-than-secluded experience, but the trail is still well worth walking. And once you start the climb to Trestle Creek Falls, any road noise falls away quickly; all you'll hear is your own labored breathing. All three of our kids backpacked the trail and camped on the creek's bank as part of a sixth-grade outdoor school experience, and all hiked up to Trestle Creek Falls. It's a challenging climb, but doable for most kids; the reward is a walk-behind waterfall and a very real sense of accomplishment.

BRICE CREEK (TRAIL SECTIONS 1.5, 2.6, AND 1.4 MILES ONE WAY; 300 FEET ELEVATION GAIN ON MIDDLE SECTION)

With four trailheads strung along the 5.5-mile trail along the creek's north bank, families have lots of options for one-way or round-trip hikes. The middle section from Cedar Creek to Lund Park offers swimming pools and a challenging climb; the easier easternmost section offers a 0.3-mile detour to Trestle Creek's 40-foot lower falls.

From the West End Trailhead, the trail rises gradually about 200 feet, veering away from the creek and into magnificent forest. In 1.5 miles pass a spur to the footbridge at Cedar Creek. From here, the trail follows the creek closely for 1 mile, passing modest Brice Creek Falls after about 0.3 mile, passing lots of inviting pools and slides, then climbs the hillside to get a good 300 feet above the creek at about 2 miles before starting back down to some primitive creekside campsites approaching the spur trail to the footbridge at Lund Park (now a trailhead and camping site with rest rooms) at 2.6 miles. There's a deep pool under the bridge that's inviting for midsummer swims. Continue on the main trail

0.6 mile to a junction with Trestle Creek Falls Trail (see below); in another 0.5 mile is the 0.3-mile detour to the misty, 40-foot Lower Trestle Creek Falls. The eastern trailhead is just 0.3 mile ahead.

UPPER TRESTLE CREEK FALLS (2 TO 2.8 MILES ROUND TRIP, 900 FEET ELEVATION GAIN)
It's a steep hike to the upper falls, but worth the effort: the forest is beautiful, and the trail leads right behind the falls, cascading down a rock cliff into a pool 100 feet below. Quickest route is a 1-mile hike from the easternmost Champion Creek Trailhead, returning for a 2-mile round trip, or continue behind the falls 1 mile down to the trail's western loop to Brice Creek Trail, turn left, and return to where you started (optional detour to the lower falls) for a 2.8-mile loop. If you start a loop hike at the Lund Park trailhead, you're in for a 3.4-mile loop.

Upper Trestle Creek Falls

 NORTH FORK TRAIL

BEFORE YOU GO
For current conditions and more information, contact Middle Fork Ranger District, *www.fs.fed.us/r6/willamette* or (541) 782-2283

ABOUT THE HIKE
Day hike
Easy to moderate for children
4.3 miles one way or 4.6 miles round trip
100 feet elevation gain
High point 1300 feet
Hikable year-round

GETTING THERE
- From Eugene take I-5 south to State Highway 58
- Just past milepost 31, turn left at the sign to Westfir and go 0.4 mile

■ Turn left and drive 1.3 miles
■ Turn left through the long red covered bridge to the trailhead parking area

HIKING THE TRAIL

Barely 45 minutes from Eugene, this newish trail on the North Fork (of the Middle Fork) of the Willamette River starts at a historic covered bridge and ends as far up the river as you care to wander. It's a great choice for spring, when water is gushing, or fall, when the big-leaf maples are turning gold. The covered bridge itself is a fun destination; cars and pedestrians are separated, so kids can explore safely.

From the trailhead, follow signs up a gravel road toward and under a railroad bridge. Bear right onto a trail where the road swings left. the trail passes briefly through a burned stretch of forest on its way into the lush forest that follows the river the rest of the way. At about 0.5 mile the trail merges with an old road for a short distance. At about 1 mile a spur trail calls you down to rocks at the edge of the river—a good spot to pause. At about 2 miles the trail leads up nearly to the road, switchbacks sharply down, then hits the road where a bridge crosses the river at 2.3 miles.

This is a good turnaround spot—if you've come this far. From here the trail resumes across the road, crossing little bridges and ascending fairly steeply (about 100 feet in elevation) to 0.6 mile before beginning a slow descent. About 0.3 before the trail ends at road 1912 at 2 miles, it crosses a substantial footbridge over Dartmouth Creek. With a shuttle car you could make a one-way hike to this point. Plans call for further extension of the trail.

Office Covered Bridge

OREGON'S HISTORIC COVERED BRIDGES

Oregon has more covered bridges than any state in the West. Early settlers built roofs over their wooden bridges' trusses to protect them from the damp weather. Most of Oregon's remaining four dozen covered bridges are in Linn and Lane Counties. The 180-foot-long Office Covered Bridge at the start of the North Fork Trail (Hike 43) is the longest in the state. It was built in 1944 by the Westfir Lumber Company to connect the company offices with the sawmill. You can see two more—Lowell and Unity Bridges—on the way from Eugene to Fall Creek (Hike 39) and another—Goodpasture Bridge—as you drive up the McKenzie River on US 126 toward hikes near McKenzie and Santiam Passes. New interpretive signs at Lowell Covered Bridge, just off State Highway 58, make it a particularly good stop.

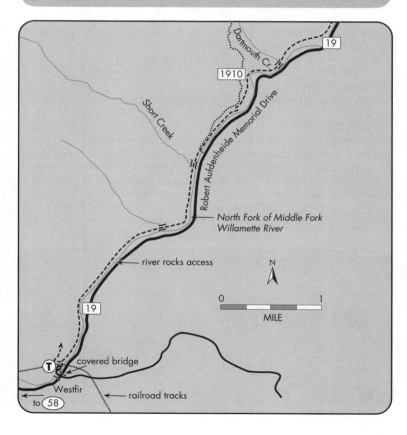

LARISON COVE

BEFORE YOU GO
For current conditions and more information, contact Middle Fork Ranger District, *www.fs.fed.us/r6/willamette* or (541) 782-2283

ABOUT THE HIKE
Day hike or backpack
Easy to moderate for children
4 miles round trip
Nearly level
High point 1600 feet
Hikable year-round

GETTING THERE
- From Eugene take I-5 south to State Highway 58
- Drive about 40 miles to the sign for Kitson Springs Road, about 1 mile east of Oakridge

- Turn south and drive 0.5 mile to Forest Road 21
- Turn right, cross the Middle Fork of the Willamette River, and bear left with the main road
- Continue 3.4 miles to the trailhead parking area on the right.

HIKING THE TRAIL
Just outside of Oakridge, Hills Creek Reservoir stretches to the south, reaching its many arms into mountain creek valleys and creating isolated coves. One particularly long cove, Larison, has an easy, quietly scenic trail following its north bank. No motorized boats are allowed on this cove. In fact, picnic areas have been developed on the south shore specifically to encourage canoeing, adding to the peaceful charm of the trail. The entire trail is more than 6 miles long, but most families will

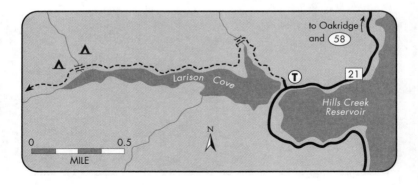

Larison Cove Trail

stop at the footbridge at the 2-mile point, near the head of the cove. Picnic here, or overnight at one of the campsites on either side of the side creek. Watch carefully for mountain bikes as you hike (though most people explore this trail on foot).

Just past the trailhead a couple of spurs lead to the water's edge; keep them in mind for cooling off on the return, though the muddy lake bottom and slight drop-off make these less-than-ideal swimming spots. Continuing up the trail, watch for poison oak. At about 0.5 mile the trail leads a short distance up a cool side-creek canyon to cross the creek on a railed log bridge. The trail then returns to the shoreline, usually staying about 50 feet above the water. Old-growth forest offers shade much of the way, though open stretches can be hot in summer.

At 2 miles the trail passes a campsite shortly before reaching a second footbridge crossing another side creek. A second campsite is just across the creek. The head of the cove, where the reservoir ends and Larison Creek begins, is about 0.2 mile beyond the footbridge, for hikers interested in more exploring.

SALT CREEK FALLS–DIAMOND CREEK FALLS

BEFORE YOU GO
For current conditions and more information, contact Middle Fork Ranger District, *www.fs.fed.us/r6/willamette* or (541) 782-2283

ABOUT THE HIKE
Day hike
Moderate for children
3.25-mile loop
450 feet elevation gain
High point 4000 feet
Hikable June through October

GETTING THERE
- From Eugene take I-5 south to State Highway 58
- Drive about 64 miles
- Immediately after a tunnel, make a sharp right onto Forest Road 5893 (just past milepost 57)
- Follow signs a short distance to the Salt Creek Falls Picnic Area

HIKING THE TRAIL
This loop hike begins and ends at one of the Northwest's most impressive waterfalls and includes another dramatic falls at the loop's far end.

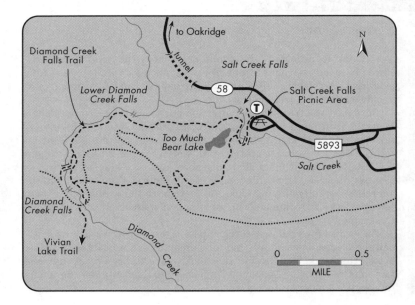

Footbridge near Salt Creek Falls

It's a fun trail with a lot of interesting stops along the way. June, with its blooming rhododendrons, is a particularly nice month for this hike.

Begin your visit with a walk down a short, paved path to view 286-foot Salt Creek Falls, which begins as a slide down a 50-foot cliff and ends with a dramatic free fall. Back at the picnic area, follow the paved path upstream a short distance to a footbridge crossing Salt Creek, then bear right. In about 50 yards signs indicate the start of the loop trail. Head counterclockwise (on Diamond Creek Falls Trail) to start the hike with a glimpse into Salt Creek Canyon from the other side of the creek.

After a short climb, the trail reaches a viewpoint atop a cliff of basalt columns. The columns create a cobblestonelike surface, interesting (and a little treacherous) for kids, given the sheer drop-off. Too Much Bear Lake lies just down the trail, off to the left; the small, oval, shallow stagnant pond was reportedly named in the 1920s by a Forest Service horse packer who had stopped here to fish.

A signed viewpoint at 0.3 mile leads to a view of the highway tunnel and sinuous creek canyon. The trail continues to roll through a forest of rhododendrons to a "viewpoint" at Lower Diamond Creek Falls at 0.7 mile. Trees obscure the view of this 200-foot falls, but this is the best view possible from the trail (though children will hear its roar as they approach and pass above it, at about 1 mile). Continue up gurgling Diamond Creek, passing a couple of clearcuts filled with rhododendrons. The trail steepens for about 0.2 mile just before, at 1.4 miles from the trailhead, it reaches the spur trail to Diamond Creek Falls. Follow this a short distance into the canyon, down a notched-log staircase, over a wide log bridge across the creek, and around the corner to see the 80-foot falls.

Back on the main trail, continue 0.2 mile to the junction with Vivian Lake Trail and bear left. Immediately cross a gravel road. From the junction, the trail mostly climbs gently for about 0.5 mile, then starts dropping through the forest of Douglas fir, hemlock, and rhododendrons, crossing the road once again. It ends back at the lower junction with Diamond Creek Falls Trail, about 1.2 miles from the upper trail junction. Continue back across Salt Creek to the picnic area.

GOING TO THE BATHROOM—WITHOUT A BATHROOM

The first Murphy's Law of Hiking with Children: Regardless of how many potty stops you make beforehand, someone has to "go" within twenty minutes of leaving the last bathroom. No problem if you're prepared. Carry a lightweight plastic trowel and two plastic self-sealing bags, one with dry toilet paper and the other to carry out used TP. You can bury the used toilet paper, but it could get dug up and scattered by animals. Some people burn their used toilet paper (risky in hot weather). It's best to treat it like any other litter and pack it out. Be sure to bury feces at least 6 inches deep, far from the trail or water sources. If you don't have a trowel, dig with a stick.

  MARILYN LAKES

BEFORE YOU GO
For current conditions and more information, contact Middle Fork Ranger District, *www.fs.fed.us/r6/willamette* or (541) 782-2283

ABOUT THE HIKE
Day hike or backpack
Easy for children
0.5 to 2 miles round trip
200 feet elevation gain
High point 5000 feet
Hikable July through October

GETTING THERE
- From Eugene take I-5 south to State Highway 58
- Drive about 68 miles to Forest Road 500 (Gold Lake Road), past milepost 61
- Turn left and follow the gravel road 1.2 miles to the lower trailhead

■ Continue 0.8 mile more to the upper trailhead at Gold Lake
Campground

HIKING THE TRAIL

Two sister lakes make a fine destination for a short hike with young
children. Walk out and back from Gold Lake (a pleasant spot for a summer camping weekend) or from the lower trailhead (just 0.25 mile from
the first lake), do a loop hike (returning on the road), or shuttle the kids
back with a one-way hike on the 1.25-mile trail. A campsite at Upper
Marilyn Lake makes an overnight trip possible.

From the lower trailhead, Upper Marilyn Lake is just 0.25 mile down
the trail through lush forest. The shore isn't particularly accessible at
this end, although it's sunny and grassy and looks inviting for picnics.
The trail gets very close to the shore as it continues around the lake's
east side. At 0.5 mile cross a short puncheon bridge over a bog. The trail
veers away from the lake, then into the woods, and hits a junction at
0.75 mile. Go left to Lower Marilyn Lake, about 150 yards away, or right
to Gold Lake, 0.5 mile farther through airy woods.

There's a campsite at Upper Marilyn Lake and what looks like the
beginning of a trail around the lake, but it fades quickly. Bushwhackers
in the group might have fun pushing farther around the lake.

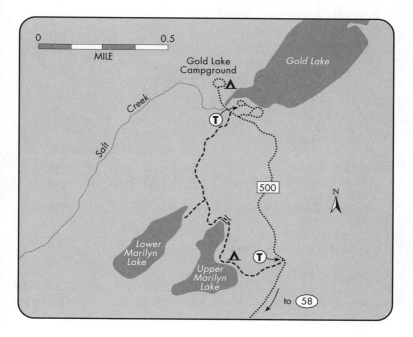

Upper Marilyn Lake

 BOBBY LAKE

BEFORE YOU GO
For current conditions and
more information, contact
Middle Fork Ranger District,
www.fs.fed.us/r6/willamette
or (541) 782-2283

ABOUT THE HIKE
Day hike or backpack
Moderate for children
4.6 miles round trip
100 feet elevation gain
High point 5600 feet
Hikable July through October

GETTING THERE
- From Eugene take I-5 south
  to State Highway 58
- Drive about 66 miles to Waldo Lake Road (Forest Road 5897) at
  milepost 59
- Turn left and drive 5.5 miles
- Park in the wide turnout on the left

HIKING THE TRAIL
Bobby Lake is one of dozens of lakes dotting the forest around Waldo Lake.
The hike in is nearly level, though rather uneventful, and the good-size
lake offers fine swimming and even decent fishing, though mosquitoes can

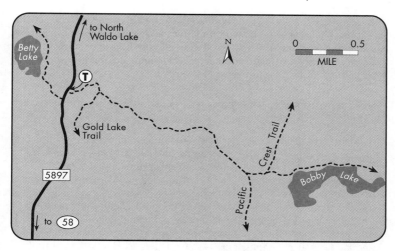

be troublesome until late July. Try to get in by late morning to soak up some sun on the big rock slab tilting into the lake's west end, or camp here and catch the morning that way. The final 0.25 mile to Bobby Lake follows a chunk of the Pacific Crest Trail (PCT); in August you may even meet up with some long-distance "through hikers" who might share some of their experiences with you.

The route to Bobby Lake begins on the east side of the road on a wide trail through airy woods; it's flat or gently rolling the entire route. At 0.4 mile you will arrive at a junction with Gold Lake Trail; go straight. The trail continues its fairly straight route, without many distractions, to its junction with the PCT at 2 miles. Turn left; the lake is ahead in 0.8 mile. Bear right at a fork to get right to the

Bobby Lake

lake; continue around to the right to get to the big rock. The trail continues along the lake's north shore and on into Deschutes National Forest. Return as you came. Back at the trailhead, any hikers needing to work off more energy can continue across the road and follow the trail to pretty Betty Lake, 0.4 mile west of the road.

SCRAM, MOSQUITOES!

Nothing can spoil a hike in the woods faster than a swarm of biting mosquitoes (especially given concerns about West Nile virus). Avoid boggy areas in spring and high mountain lakes early in summer. The best defense is a chemical repellent of some kind. "Natural" repellents with ingredients such as citronella sometimes work, though they may require frequent reapplication to be of any use. Otherwise virtually all repellents use the chemical N, N-diethyl-m-toluamide, nicknamed DEET, as the active ingredient, in concentrations as high as 95 percent. Avoid the higher concentrations; they've been linked to serious health problems and are especially not advised for young children. (I've seen them melt paint and smear the color in vinyl car seats.) And high concentrations of DEET are not much more effective than the low concentrations of about 6.5 percent, though you may have to reapply these more frequently. Wearing a long-sleeved shirt and long pants helps as well.

---

48 SOUTH WALDO SHELTER

BEFORE YOU GO
For current conditions and more information, contact Middle Fork Ranger District, *www.fs.fed.us/r6/willamette* or (541) 782-2283

ABOUT THE HIKE
Day hike or backpack
Easy to moderate for children
3.4 miles round trip
Nearly level
High point 5400 feet
Hikable July through October

GETTING THERE

- From Eugene take I-5 south to State Highway 58
- Drive about 66 miles to Waldo Lake Road (Forest Road 5897) at milepost 59
- Drive 7 miles to Forest Road 5896
- Turn left at the sign to Shadow Bay Campground, and follow signs to the boat ramp

South Waldo Shelter

HIKING THE TRAIL

At 10 square miles, Waldo Lake is the second-largest lake in Oregon and is considered by scientists to be perhaps the purest large lake in the world. It's a grand place in late summer, when the swarms of mosquitoes that plague campers in early summer are gone. A 21.8-mile trail encircles the entire lake; this short, level stretch offers excellent views of the lake and nice camping.

A trail sign points toward the bay, where a crescent of smooth, white sand beckons. If hikers can tear themselves away, pick up the trail heading south, following it around Shadow Bay and crossing a couple of small bridges in the process. At 0.4 mile the trail joins the main Waldo Lake Trail and, shortly thereafter, enters Waldo Lake Wilderness.

About this point, pause to see if anything seems different. It should: The trail is now beyond the protection of the bay, and even on a gentle day hikers should be feeling the wind across the lake and seeing waves lapping at the shore. Soon the trail crosses a substantial footbridge, then leads through a bog filled with skunk cabbage and, at 1 mile, crosses another beefy bridge, and then another.

Here look for a particularly pretty beach; on hot summer days, its gentle surf is reminiscent of a tropical beach. Eventually the terrain becomes more rolling, and at about 1.3 miles the trail swings out of sight of the lake to skirt a marsh. Cross one more big footbridge before reaching three-sided, shingle-roofed South Waldo Shelter at 1.7 miles.

The meadows here are inviting for camping, and the shelter itself might be a godsend on a rainy day. There are no bunks or stove, but

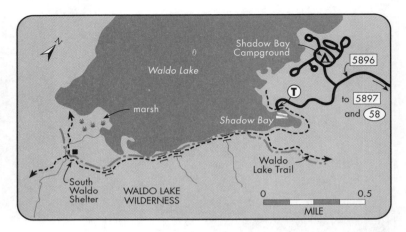

there's a fireplace in front. Turn around here or continue farther up the trail. Waldo Lake comes back into view in about 0.3 mile.

 ISLET BEACH

BEFORE YOU GO
For current conditions and more information, contact Middle Fork Ranger District, www.fs.fed.us/r6/willamette or (541) 782-2283

ABOUT THE HIKE
Day hike or backpack
Easy for children
2.5 miles round trip
Nearly level
High point 5400 feet
Hikable July through October

GETTING THERE

- From Eugene take I-5 south to State Highway 58
- Drive about 66 miles to Waldo Lake Road (Forest Road 5897) at milepost 59
- Drive 13 miles (becomes Forest Road 5898)
- Turn left at the sign to Islet Campground
- Follow signs 1.2 miles to the boat ramp and trailhead sign

HIKING THE TRAIL
Waldo Lake offers several swimming beaches accessible by road; Islet Beach requires a hike—a short one that's worth every step. A long, wide crescent of soft sand faces west and, on sunny days, is bathed in sun all

Islet Beach

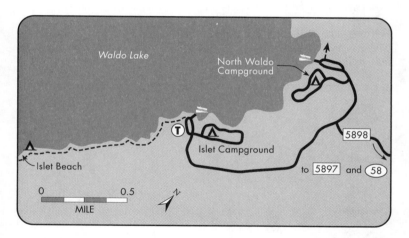

afternoon long. The hike is an easy stroll through the woods, past several smaller beaches and coves—warm-up acts to the main event. Wait to visit until late July, when mosquitoes are fewer.

Hike south on the shoreline trail. (The main Waldo Lake Trail circling the lake is far from the lake at this point.) Immediately the trail passes a small gray-sand beach, then a small cove at 0.2 mile, then another small beach at 0.9 mile—all worth a stop. The trail ends at Islet Beach, some 75 sandy yards long. Look for a campsite on a promontory overlooking the lake just north of the beach. Return as you came.

ROSARY LAKES

BEFORE YOU GO
For current conditions and more information, contact Middle Fork Ranger District, *www.fs.fed.us/r6/willamette* or (541) 782-283

ABOUT THE HIKE
Day hike or backpack
Challenging for children
7 miles round trip
800 feet elevation gain
High point 5880 feet
Hikable July through October

GETTING THERE
- From Eugene take I-5 south to State Highway 58
- Drive about 69 miles to Willamette Pass (milepost 62)
- Just past the ski area, turn left (may be marked with hiker sign)
- Bear right at the highway maintenance shed and gravel pit
- Park at the trailhead at the far end of the parking area

HIKING THE TRAIL
The Rosary Lakes, just east of the crest of the Cascades, are what they sound like: a succession of three emerald lakes strung close together in

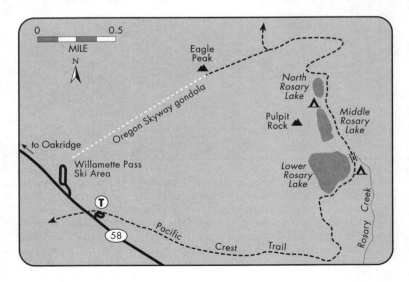

Opposite: Middle Rosary Lake

deep forest. The most difficult part of the hike is the initial 2.7 miles to the first lake; it's not steep, just long and not terribly interesting. If kids are old enough to handle a hike this long, they'll be glad they did: the closely set lakes are fun for brisk dips and even trout fishing. Carry river shoes to wear into the muddy lakes.

The route follows the Pacific Crest Trail through an airy pine-and-fir forest on a gentle but steady incline; watch for glimpses of Odell Lake through the trees to the south. At 2.7 miles you'll reach the shore of Lower Rosary Lake, a medium-size mountain lake with a scree slope on its far side. The trail continues around the lake's gentle south shore, passing campsites on a flat above the lake. At 3 miles cross a bridge over the lower lake's outlet, then start uphill toward Middle Rosary Lake, about 0.4 mile farther. North Rosary Lake is at 3.5 miles, just across a narrow band of forest from its sister. Return as you came.

With the Oregon Skyway gondola operating at Willamette Pass ski area in the summer, hikers have another option: a one-way, 6-mile, all-downhill walk past the Rosary Lakes from the top of 6683-foot Eagle Peak. The Skyway is also popular with sightseers and mountain bikers, though cyclists cannot use the Pacific Crest Trail to the Rosary Lakes. The Skyway opens up other all-downhill day hiking possibilities as well. Visit *www.willamettepass.com* for prices and schedule.

Opposite: View from Grizzly Peak Trail

SOUTHERN CASCADES AND **SISKIYOUS**

 **FERN FALLS**

ABOUT THE HIKE
Day hike
Easy for children
3.5 miles round trip
Nearly level
High point 840 feet
Hikable year-round

GETTING THERE

- From Roseburg, take State Highway 138 east about 21 miles
- Turn south at Swiftwater Bridge, west of milepost 22

HIKING THE TRAIL

The 76-mile North Umpqua Trail is one of several long-distance riverside trails in western Oregon. The lower end of the trail is particularly appealing to families, as it provides year-round hiking opportunities on gentle grades. Here the trail follows the river's south bank, opposite State Highway 138; road bridges at four points divide the trail into three sections ranging from 5 miles to 15.7 miles in length.

The lowest section is too long of a day hike for most people (15.7 miles). However, it lends itself to an out-and-back hike to Fern Falls that's accessible all year. From Swiftwater Bridge, hike upstream on the nearly level trail 0.25 mile to a spur on the left, leading to a view of Deadline Falls. Here, especially from May through September, watch for

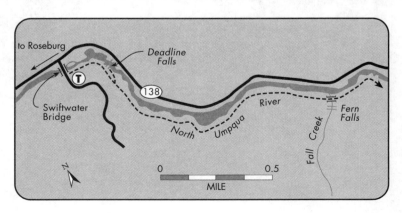

Fern Falls

anadromous (migrating) fish—Chinook and coho salmon, plus steelhead
trout—attempting to jump the falls. The trail continues into a gorgeous
forest dripping with moss, crossing little side creeks. You will discover
many places to scramble down to the rushing North Umpqua River.
Stay on the lookout for poison oak all along the trail. At 1.75 miles the
trail crosses Fall Creek on a laminated wood footbridge at Fern Falls.
Under the bridge, the creek spreads out in a shallow, rocky fan, inviting
for water play. Continue up the trail, or turn around and return the way
you came.

SUSAN CREEK FALLS

BEFORE YOU GO
For current conditions and more information, contact Bureau of Land Management, Roseburg, www.blm.gov/or/districts /roseburg or (541) 672-4491

ABOUT THE HIKE
Day hike
Easy for children
1 mile round trip
120 feet elevation gain
High point 1060 feet
Hikable year-round

GETTING THERE
- From Roseburg, take State Highway 138 east about 27 miles
- Park at the Susan Creek picnic area on the south side of the highway

HIKING THE TRAIL
The North Umpqua corridor offers a wealth of short waterfall hikes, ideal for families with young children. As an alternative to one long day hike, consider driving up State Highway 138, stopping to take in two or three short hikes. Put Susan Creek Falls at the top of your list. From Roseburg you can drive to the trailhead in about a half-hour, and its low elevation means spring and its wildflowers come early.

The trail starts across the highway from the picnic area. Follow it through deep forest east of the creek. The trail ends at the base of the

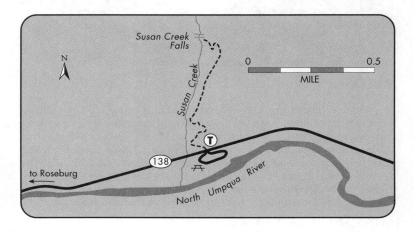

Susan Creek

falls, which tumbles 60 feet into a punch bowl. Look for dippers, or water ouzels—small, dark-gray birds adapted to life in and around mountain streams. They often build nests right on the edge of waterfalls, and they're frequently seen at Susan Creek Falls dipping in the spray and walking under the stream. Return as you came.

 FALL CREEK FALLS

BEFORE YOU GO
For current conditions and more information, contact North Umpqua Ranger District, *www.fs.fed.us/r6/umpqua* or (541) 496-3532

ABOUT THE HIKE
Day hike
Easy for children
1.8 miles round trip
380 feet elevation gain
High point 1400 feet
Hikable year-round

GETTING THERE
- From Roseburg, take State Highway 138 east about 32 miles
- Park at the signed trailhead parking lot on the left

HIKING THE TRAIL
It's easy to keep kids interested along this short trail, from the wooden bridge at the trailhead to the viewing platform partway up the falls. Spring brings an array of woodland wildflowers to the trail's borders, further enhancing a hike here.

From the trailhead, immediately cross Fall Creek on a wooden bridge,

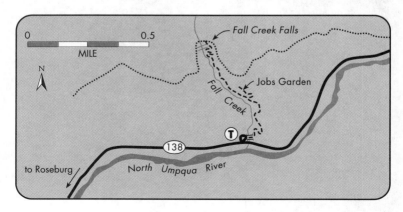

Fall Creek Falls

then pass through a cut in a tree that appears to have fallen across the trail—an opportunity to talk about assessing a tree's age from the growth rings. (Too many to count them all? Count back from the edge to find the ring that, had the tree fallen today, would indicate the years your kids were born.)

Just up the trail, squeeze through a crevice in a rock the size of a small house. The trail continues close to the creek, which spills and froths over mossy boulders. It switchbacks uphill briefly; then, at about 0.5 mile, a spur trail takes off to the right, leading in 0.1 mile to Jobs Garden (an area of unusual rock formations). There's plenty of poison oak here, so watch the children and stay on the trail. As the creek flattens, the trail levels out and veers away from it, still staying within earshot.

At about 0.8 mile the trail rejoins the creek, now flat and quiet, just before reaching the falls. Here the creek twists around a corner, then showers down a rock face, falling nearly 100 feet in the process. **Caution:** A slippery log crosses the creek just downstream of the falls—fun to walk on, but hazardous without close supervision. The trail continues up the hill next to the falls, switchbacking four more times to the top of the falls. There's not much to see at the top, though there's a nice intermediate viewpoint along the way. The trail ends at a gravel road atop the falls. Return as you came.

POISON OAK MYTHS AND FACTS

Poison oak is a shrub found along many trails in southern Oregon as well as in the southern Willamette Valley and parts of the south coast. It's known by its glossy three-part leaves and the rash caused by those sensitive to the urushiol oil found in its leaves, stalks, and roots. If it doesn't bother you, you're lucky! The rest of us can look forward to an icky, oozing rash lasting 10 days to two weeks. If you've touched poison oak, wash yourself well with soap (there are special soaps to get rid of the urushiol) and wash any clothes that may have brushed up against it. Wash your dog, too. But don't worry about "contaminating" other people with your rash, nor about spreading it by scratching. It can only be spread by exposure to the urushiol oil.

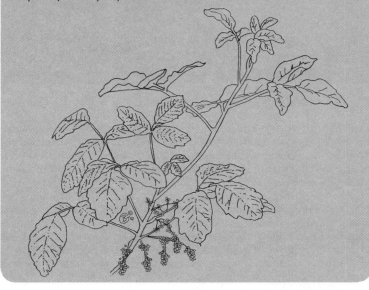

TOKETEE AND WATSON FALLS

BEFORE YOU GO
For current conditions and more information, contact Diamond Lake Ranger District, *www.fs.fed.us/r6/umpqua* or (541) 498-2531

ABOUT THE HIKE
Day hike
Easy for children
1 mile round trip each
100 to 280 feet elevation gain
High point 3040 feet
Hikable most of the year

GETTING THERE

- From Roseburg, take State Highway 138 east about 55 miles
- Turn north at the west entrance to Toketee Ranger Station (milepost 59)
- Turn left and cross a bridge
- Turn left again onto a gravel road
- Continue a short distance to the trailhead for Toketee Falls
- To **Watson Falls:** Take State 138 about 2 miles farther. Turn right on Forest Road 37 (between mileposts 61 and 62). Drive 0.1 mile to the large, signed parking area on the right

HIKING THE TRAIL

Trailheads for these two short hikes are just about 2 miles apart; pair them and you'll have 2 miles of hiking and some of southern Oregon's best waterfall views. Toketee Falls is probably the most dramatic of the North Umpqua corridor falls, especially viewed as hikers do—across a

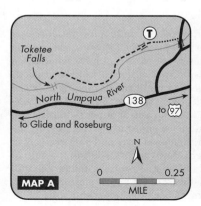

Watson Falls

chasm from a platform clinging to a cliff. Children will enjoy watching the water burble and swirl in the creek alongside the trail as it approaches the falls. The narrow tread and steep drop-offs urge caution with young children, however.

TOKETEE FALLS

That huge, dripping redwood pipe you see next to the trailhead is used to divert water from nearby Toketee Lake and carry it to another pipe, where it drops steeply to a powerhouse to make electricity. Cross a footbridge and walk the level path through the forest, passing several potential picnic sites along the river. The trail then starts to climb a bit on sturdy stone steps. Peek down to the left at the gorgeous deep pools in the creek along the trail. Hikers may want to wander off the trail to play in a safe spot along the creek. Approaching the end, the trail drops about 100 feet to a viewing platform perched on the side of the canyon. Look across a wide gulf to see the North Umpqua River pouring through a cleft in a wall of columnar basalt and dropping some 90 feet into an emerald pool. Return as you came.

WATSON FALLS

Signs lead hikers up across Forest Road 37 and onto a footpath ascending the hillside across the road. The route is rather steep, sticking close to the creek as it runs noisily over mossy boulders that have rolled down out of the mountains. The first trailside view of the falls comes at about 0.25 mile. Keep going to a railed wooden platform zigzagging over the creek near the base of the falls. Continue up the trail on another switchback for a better view of the falls, then up yet another switchback to reach the highest viewpoint, poised about one-third of the way up the falls in a magnificent natural amphitheater of gray and pale green rock and moss. The cataract falls straight down a cliff, pounding a pile of boulders and vaporizing into clouds of mist. To return, follow signs to the "return trail" spur that starts just west of the railed platform bridge. It takes a slightly steeper, quicker route back to the parking area.

CLEETWOOD COVE

ABOUT THE HIKE
Day hike
Moderate for children
2.2 miles round trip
760 feet elevation gain
High point 6935 feet
Hikable July through October
FYI no dogs allowed

GETTING THERE
- From Medford, take State Highway 62 about 70 miles north to the western border of Crater Lake National Park

- Continue east on State 62 about 7 miles
- Turn left toward park headquarters and drive 4 miles to Rim Drive
- Turn left and drive 3 miles to Rim Village
- Continue north and then east on Rim Drive 10.6 miles more
- Park in the large trailhead parking area on the left side of the road

HIKING THE TRAIL
Thousands of people drive around the rim of Crater Lake, gazing across its deep, clear blue waters, but far fewer actually dip their toes in it. There's only one way to get to the lake, and that's with a hike down the Cleetwood Trail. Boat tours to Wizard Island leave from the dock at the trail's end; call park headquarters for the schedule. Even without

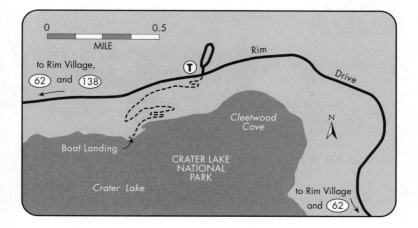

Cleetwood Cove dock on Crater Lake

the boat ride, the hike is worthwhile, especially if it's hot enough to justify a dive or a dip into the bone-chilling lake.

Cross the road to reach the trailhead. The wide trail's descent isn't really steep, but it's steady. Benches are scattered all along the trail. (The prospect of a boat tour motivates a lot of less-than-fit tourists to walk this trail; they make good use of the opportunities to rest on the return.) The lake glimmers along the trail all the way down the long switchbacks. The trail ends at the little boat dock. Sit on the edge of the dock, dipping your feet, or pick your way along the boulder-strewn shore to find a picnic or wading spot. Bring old sneakers or aqua socks for wading, as the rocks can be sharp.

A boat tour here is a great way to learn about the geologic forces that created Crater Lake and the landmarks around the rim. At Wizard Island you can get out and hike 0.9 mile (and 764 feet) up to the top of the island, catching another boat to return—assuming there's room; it's a little chancy (see Hike 56 map).

56 THE WATCHMAN

BEFORE YOU GO
For current conditions and more information, contact Crater Lake National Park, *www.nps.gov/crla* or (541) 594-2211

ABOUT THE HIKE
Day hike
Easy to moderate for children
1.4 miles round trip
420 feet elevation gain
High point 8056 feet
Hikable July through October
FYI no dogs allowed

GETTING THERE
- From Medford, take State Highway 62 about 70 miles north to the western border of Crater Lake National Park

- Continue east on State 62 about 7 miles
- Turn left toward park headquarters and drive 4 miles to Rim Drive
- Turn left and drive 3 miles to Rim Village
- Continue north on Rim Drive 3.8 miles
- Park in the viewpoint parking area for The Watchman

HIKING THE TRAIL

Don't visit Crater Lake without hiking up to a high point overlooking the lake. Several peaks with summit trails dot the rim. The Watchman is the shortest and easiest of the bunch, and still grants a dynamite bird's-eye view of the deep blue lake and the best view of Wizard Island, directly below.

The trail starts just south of the parking area along the rim. Climb a long straightaway that gradually curves behind The Watchman peak. At about 0.5 mile the trail reaches a switchback—the first of a half-dozen switchbacks that come closer and closer together as you near the top. At the summit there's a fire lookout cabin, but no visitors are allowed inside. (With so many visitors, the person staffing the lookout would never get a chance to watch for fires.) Instead enjoy the view from the rock-walled viewpoint. Return as you came.

Older children seeking more challenge might enjoy Garfield Peak, a 3-mile round trip (980 feet elevation gain) that begins just behind Crater Lake Lodge, or Mount Scott, a 5-mile round trip (1326 feet elevation gain) directly across the lake from Rim Village.

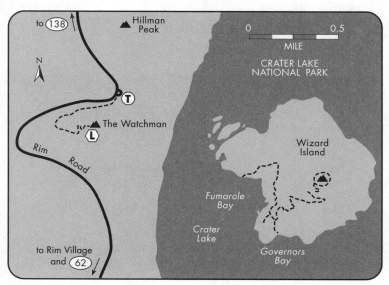

Lookout atop The Watchman

GOOD TRAIL MANNERS

Follow these guidelines to preserve the environment and ensure a good experience for other hikers.

- **Don't litter.** Better yet, bring an extra plastic bag to bring out others' trash you might find.
- **Don't pick anything.** Leave the flowers—and for that matter, the colorful mushrooms and the hermit crabs—to live out their natural lives and to let others enjoy seeing them.
- **Stay on the trail,** rather than cutting across switchbacks, which leads to erosion.
- **Don't camp on lakeshores** or in other delicate environments.
- **Keep dogs on leash if there are other hikers around.** It's required in wilderness areas and on certain other trails.

UNION CREEK

BEFORE YOU GO
For current conditions and more information, contact Prospect Ranger District, *www .fs.fed.us/r6/rogue-siskiyou* or (541) 560-3400

ABOUT THE HIKE
Day hike
Easy to moderate for children
4.4 miles one way
Gentle ascent or descent (445 feet elevation gain)
High point 3765 feet
Hikable April through November

GETTING THERE
- From Medford, take State Highway 62 north about 55 miles to the community of Union Creek
- To reach the upper trailhead, continue north 3.3 miles to Forest Road 600
- Turn right and drive 0.2 mile to Forest Road 610
- Bear left and continue 0.2 mile to the trailhead, on the right

HIKING THE TRAIL
The charm of Union Creek Trail sneaks up on you. There are no dramatic vistas, just easy walking through a magnificent forest following a babbling creek. Start a one-way hike at the upper end with a splash (a view of pretty Union Falls) and end at the community of Union Creek. Or begin

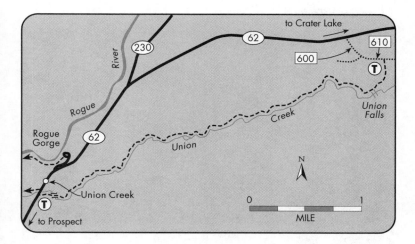

at Union Creek and wander upstream a mile or two, then turn around. In addition to huge, old-growth Douglas fir, there are hemlocks, sugar pines, alder, yew, and all kinds of wildflowers in late spring.

The lower trailhead is on the south side of the highway bridge over the creek at the community of Union Creek. Follow the path up the east bank a short distance, cross the creek on a footbridge (slippery when wet), and continue up the west bank. Starting at the upper trailhead, walk through the level forest, listening for falls, then drop down the hillside to reach the base of Union Falls at 0.3 mile. Here the creek drops about 5 feet over a smooth lip, then churns and boils down several more ledges.

From the falls, the trail winds gently down along the north bank of Union Creek, usually in sight of the wide creek. Notice the moss-covered volcanic creek bed at the upper end; farther down, as the lava diminishes, the creek's edges are less well defined. Logs are strewn across the creek in many places, creating tempting footbridges and obscuring the creek in places. Point out to children the midstream islands; some appear to have started after a tree fell into the creek and other plants began to grow on the decaying tree. They also can see dry channels where apparently the creek was diverted by a logjam. What caused all those logs to fall into the creek? Logging operations, beavers, wind, and even the creek itself, undercutting the root systems of trees along its bank.

After crossing the footbridge back at Union Creek, the trail reaches the highway at 4.4 miles, but it continues across the road another 0.4 mile to intersect the Rogue Gorge Trail. You'll want to visit Rogue Gorge while you're in the area; a short asphalt path leads past dramatic views of the Rogue River churning its way through a narrow lava chasm. Fencing and viewing platforms make it safe for even young children.

Union Creek Trail

NATURAL BRIDGE

BEFORE YOU GO
For current conditions and more information, contact Prospect Ranger District, *www.fs.fed.us/r6/rogue-siskiyou* or (541) 560-3400

ABOUT THE HIKE
Day hike
Easy for children
2-mile loop
200 feet elevation gain
High point 3200 feet
Hikable April through November

GETTING THERE
- From Medford, take State Highway 62 north about 54 miles (1 mile south of Union Creek)
- Turn left at the sign to Natural Bridge (Forest Road 300) and continue 0.5 mile
- Bear left at the Y
- Park at the day-use area

HIKING THE TRAIL
In its dash from the slopes of Crater Lake's Mount Mazama to the Pacific Ocean, the Rogue River does a sudden disappearing act, reappearing a

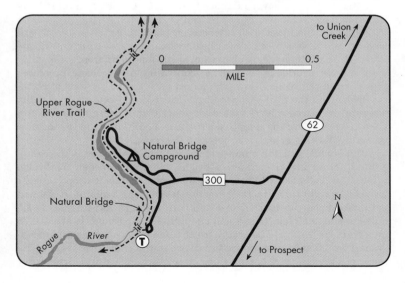

Footbridge at Natural Bridge, Rogue River

short distance downstream. Where did it go? Into a series of lava tubes in the river's channel. An excellent interpretive trail overlooking Natural Bridge enlightens visitors and steers them safely away from walking on Natural Bridge itself. Link that short, paved path with forest trails on either side of the river, throw in a pair of footbridges, and what results is a wonderful, generally uncrowded loop hike. The east-bank trail section skirts a busy campground, but the west-bank section is little used.

The trail is generally snow-free from April through November, but the road to Natural Bridge is open only mid-May through mid-October. It's possible to catch the loop by walking the 0.5 mile in from the highway or, better yet, hiking down 1.5 miles from Union Creek on the east-bank trail. You may even have the entire trail to yourself.

Walk past the kiosk with interpretive signs to get on a paved path leading to a dramatic metal footbridge spanning the churning Rogue River. The path then winds upstream, safely fenced off from steep cliffs, with several overlooks and signs explaining the geologic processes that created the scene below. The paved path ends at a view of Natural Bridge, but the trail—Upper Rogue River Trail—continues as a dirt footpath. It follows a level course for about 0.25 mile, then climbs perhaps 200 feet above the river in deep woods. Look down and see the now peacefully flowing green river between the trees.

After a while you will glimpse tents and trailers parked in the campground across the river, then a bright, bleached, wooden footbridge below. The trail seems to overshoot the footbridge as it drops to river level, but a right turn at a trail junction leads along a quaint, rock-lined path back to the bridge. Cross it and turn right. (A left turn leads 1.5 miles to Union Creek.) The north end of the campground is about 0.25 mile from the bridge. The trail here threads between river and campground for 0.5 mile or so; notice the river's initial calm, then its growing sense of urgency, as it narrows and drops toward Natural Bridge. For the last 0.25 mile the trail veers away from the river and into the woods, ending at the viewpoint parking area.

 TAKELMA GORGE

BEFORE YOU GO
For current conditions and more information, contact Prospect Ranger District, *www .fs.fed.us/r6/rogue-siskiyou* or (541) 560-3400

ABOUT THE HIKE
Day hike
Moderate for children
2.8 to 3.8 miles round trip
120 feet elevation gain
High point 2960 feet
Hikable most of the year

GETTING THERE
- From Medford, take State Highway 62 about 50 miles (4.7 miles south of Union Creek)
- Turn left at the sign to Woodruff Bridge (Forest Road 68)
- Drive 2 miles
- Park on the left just before the bridge

HIKING THE TRAIL
The 48-mile-long Upper Rogue River Trail follows the river from the town of Prospect upstream to Crater Rim Viewpoint, just outside Crater Lake National Park, providing a lot of options for relatively easy one-way and round-trip hikes. Two of those options appear in this book: Hike 58 (Natural Bridge Loop) and this one, a hike to dramatic Takelma Gorge. From Woodruff Bridge, hike out to the gorge and back; alternately, leave a shuttle car at River Bridge Campground and hike 4.6 miles one way from Woodruff Bridge.

Start by heading south on Upper Rogue River Trail; the river reappears in 0.25 mile, flowing

Takelma Gorge

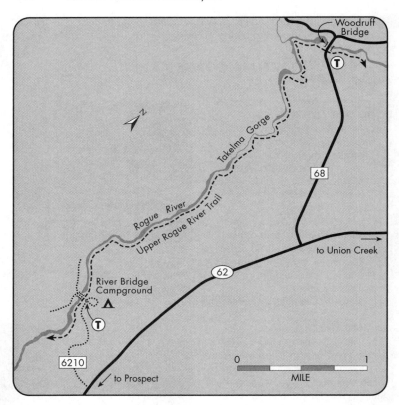

placidly here. The trail continues downstream, mostly level with a few ups and downs, with the river mostly out of sight. At about 1 mile the river can be heard and seen quickening its pace, as if it were anticipating the gorge ahead. The trail grows rockier where it passes atop basalt-column cliffs; look across the river to see similar cliffs. Is this the gorge? Not quite; it's obvious when it appears. Continue another 0.4 mile and there it is: a channel of white water turning sharply and roaring between vertical cliffs of dark basalt, under logs swept downstream and lodged between the gorge walls.

Turn around here or continue along the top of the 0.5-mile gorge before returning. Below the gorge the river flattens again, and it's a mellow 2.5 miles to River Bridge Campground. To leave a car at this end, take State 62 south 2.2 miles from the Woodruff Bridge turnoff, turn right on gravel Road 6210, and follow it 1 mile to the campground.

UPPER TABLE ROCK

BEFORE YOU GO
For current conditions and more information, contact Bureau of Land Management, Medford, (541) 770-2200

ABOUT THE HIKE
Day hike
Moderate for children
2.5 miles round trip
800 feet elevation gain
High point 2050 feet
Hikable year-round
FYI no camping, no dogs allowed

GETTING THERE
- From I-5 in Medford take exit 33 (Central Point)
- Follow Biddle Road 0.8 mile to Table Rock Road
- Turn left and drive 5.3 miles
- Where the road swings to the left, turn right on Modoc Road
- Continue 1.5 miles to the signed trailhead, on the left

HIKING THE TRAIL
Anyone who has driven past Medford on I-5 has noticed the pair of flattop mesas north of the freeway. Both Upper and Lower Table Rock have trails to their summits; the trail that ascends Upper Table Rock is shorter, a little less steep, and a bit more open for views. It's a good wildflower walk in spring, but children will be more intrigued by the summit, which is literally flat enough to land a plane on. The grassy summit is a bit boggy in winter and spring; in summer, go early in the day, before the heat

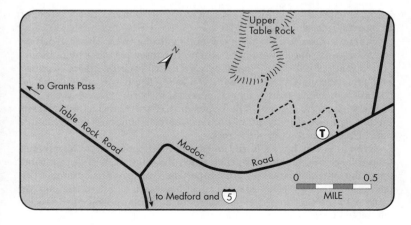

Upper Table Rock

becomes oppressive. In all seasons, beware of poison oak and (according to reports) rattlesnakes.

Start up through a tangle of oak and madrona trees. The trail can be rocky in some places, muddy in others. It passes between huge basalt outcrops at 0.2 mile. At 0.5 mile there's a bench inviting hikers to pause and enjoy the view of the Rogue River Valley. There's another bench at 0.9 mile, where the trail enters the forest and obscures the view the rest of the way to the summit. The upper part of the trail has some steep pitches. Quite suddenly, at 1.25 miles, the trail emerges onto the flat, open expanse at the top of the rock.

Even kids who have a hard time dragging themselves to the summit tend to become converts once they reach the summit, with its unusual open, flat, virtually treeless landscape. The trail hits the summit near one end of the horseshoe-shaped rock; head left to get to the end, or wander to the center of the horseshoe for a dramatic view of the rocky gorge below. Return as you came.

OREGON CAVES–BIG TREE LOOP

BEFORE YOU GO
For current conditions and
more information, contact
Oregon Caves National
Monument, *www.nps.gov/orca*
or (541) 592-2100

ABOUT THE HIKE
Day hike
Moderate for children
3.3-mile loop
1100 feet elevation gain
High point 5080 feet
Hikable July through October

GETTING THERE

- From US Highway 199 in
  Cave Junction, turn east onto
  State Highway 46
- Drive 19 miles to the parking lot at Oregon Caves National
  Monument

HIKING THE TRAIL
Hikers in southern Oregon don't tend to think of the trails around
Oregon Caves National Monument when choosing a destination, and
tourists visiting the caves don't tend to be interested in hiking. The

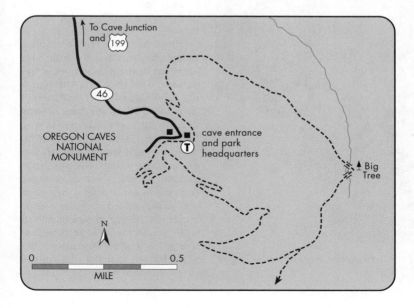

combination makes this interesting and moderately challenging loop trail uncrowded as well, despite its proximity to a popular tourist attraction. This hike, along with a tour of the caves, makes a full day's outing for a family. The complete loop is 3.3 miles, but an out-and-back hike to the huge Douglas fir is only 2.6 miles. Ask at the monument's information office about even shorter loop hikes in the caves area.

Walk up the road toward the cave entrance, then continue up the double staircases, past the ticket booth, and onto an asphalt path. Immediately the trail splits, signaling the start of the loop trail. Turn left for a more gradual approach to the Big Tree.

The trail quickly turns to dirt. The route, fairly steep for the first 0.4 mile, flattens out for a bit where the first of several trailside benches appears. Then the trail makes a turn to the right; notice how the trees are bigger here and the forest cooler. At about 0.7 mile the trail gets steeper again and heads up steadily. In early July some pink rhododendrons may be in bloom. At 1.3 miles cross a tiny creek and immediately reach the Big Tree—a twelve-and-a-half-foot-thick Douglas fir.

From here the trail continues up steadily another 0.4 mile to a junction; bear right and begin the descent. The trail cuts through a moist hillside where a profusion of flowers crowding the trail blooms in early summer; if the day is wet, hikers' legs will be, too. Swing down through the old-growth forest on long switchbacks. Suddenly, at about 3 miles, the trail emerges from the forest to offer a view over the shake-roofed Oregon Caves buildings, silvery in sunlight. The trail passes a couple of interpretive signs before turning to asphalt for the last 0.2 mile to the caves entrance area.

Early spring snow outside Oregon Caves

TWO VERY DIFFERENT KINDS OF CAVES

Oregon hikers can explore two very different kinds of underground caves. The caverns at Oregon Caves National Monument (near Hike 61) in southern Oregon are marble caves formed over thousands of years by acidic water slowly seeping into an area of limestone rock, dissolving calcium carbonate (the main ingredient in limestone) and building calcite formations called stalagmites and stalagtites. If you visit the caves, notice the water present throughout the caves. The lava tubes of Central Oregon, such as Lava River Cave (Hike 72) have a completely different origin. They were formed quickly when a flow of hot lava, in this case from Newberry Volcano, began to cool and crusted over. The lava inside the flow drained out, leaving an empty tube. The "river" refers to the river of lava; geologists believe no river of water ever flowed in the cave.

 RAINIE FALLS

BEFORE YOU GO
For current conditions and more information, contact Smullen Visitor Center at Rand, www.blm.gov/or/resources /recreation/rogue/rogue _river.htm or (541) 479-3735

ABOUT THE HIKE
Day hike or backpack
Easy to moderate for children
3.6 miles round trip
700 feet elevation gain
High point 790 feet
Hikable year-round

GETTING THERE
- From I-5 just north of Grants Pass, take exit 61 (Merlin)
- Follow Merlin-Galice Road west 25 miles
- Cross Grave Creek Bridge
- Take the spur road to the boat landing and trailhead on the left

HIKING THE TRAIL
A wilderness river alternating between placid pools and wild white water, old cabins and archeological sites, gushing side creek waterfalls, and a benign climate are just a few of the attractions of the 40-mile Rogue River Trail. It's not as level as some riverside trails, but neither is it difficult, and attractions all along the way keep children interested—as long as the hike isn't attempted at midday in midsummer. Late spring is the ideal season to

Trail post along Rogue River Trail

hike the Rogue River Trail. You may experience some showers or even a real storm, but weather tends to be pleasantly sunny and warm. If you're planning an overnight trek, make arrangements with the nearby Galice Resort to have your car shuttled back to Galice; it's illegal, and unwise, to leave a car at the landing overnight.

Rainie Falls makes a good destination for a short hike with children out of Grants Pass. Trails lead down both sides of the river from Grave Creek, where rafters put in for multiday trips into the wild canyon. From the boat landing, the Rogue River Trail starts up steeply, along a sheer slope overlooking the river, then levels out. At 0.6 mile look around to see the remains of an old miner's cabin. You will see another cabin across the river at 1.3 miles. Notice the concrete pier here; it was part of a stock bridge built in 1907 but destroyed in the flood of 1927. At 1.8 miles the trail reaches Rainie Falls, a dramatic 15- to 20-foot drop in the river. Hang around and you may see a party of boaters use ropes to line

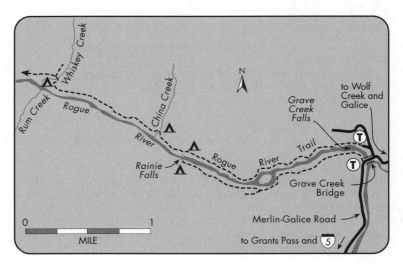

their rafts or drift boats down the narrow, more gradual channel along the north bank. A spur trail to the camping area is 0.1 mile back upstream.

Want more walking? Go another 1.5 miles to Whiskey Creek. The broad meadow and beach make it an appealing spot for a picnic and a popular spot for camping. There's another camping area 0.4 mile downstream, the last one for 2 miles. Check at Smullen Visitor Center, along the river between Galice and Grave Creek, for information about long-distance hikes or float trips down the Rogue.

Alternately, walk the 2-mile south bank trail to the trail's end at Rainie Falls—a slightly rockier, rougher trail with some switchbacks, but one ending with an even better view of the falls. You can park at the pullout at the east end of Grave Creek Bridge.

 GRIZZLY PEAK

BEFORE YOU GO
For current conditions and more information, contact Bureau of Land Management, Medford, www.blm.gov/or/districts/medford or (541) 618-2200

ABOUT THE HIKE
Day hike
Moderate for children
4.8-mile loop
680 feet elevation gain
High point 5922 feet
Hikable May to October

GETTING THERE

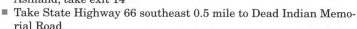

- From I-5 at the south end of Ashland, take exit 14
- Take State Highway 66 southeast 0.5 mile to Dead Indian Memorial Road
- Turn left and drive 6.7 miles to Shale City Road (BLM Road 38-2E-27)
- Turn left and drive 3 miles to BLM Road 38-2E-9.2
- Turn left and drive 0.8 mile to a five-way intersection with power lines overhead
- Take the upper of two left forks onto gravel Road 39-2E-9.2
- Continue 1 mile to the trailhead at road's end

HIKING THE TRAIL
From downtown Ashland, look across the valley to the northeast, up to twin humps on the horizon scattered with gray snags—the remains of a forest fire on Grizzly Peak. An ascent to viewpoints on the peak is doable for moderately fit kids, rewarding with a riot of wildflowers in midsummer and views of the Ashland valley below and Mount Ashland and Mount

Grizzly Peak

Shasta beyond. The Antelope Fire burned through here in 2002; the mostly gentle loop trail now winds alternately through lush conifer groves and dramatic burned but recovering forest.

The trail immediately heads up, ascending 1.1 miles through a Douglas fir, white fir, and hemlock forest to a junction. Go left for a quicker out-and-back hike to the best viewpoint (1 mile ahead). To hike the loop, go right instead, passing the peak's rock-pile summit on your right in a scant 0.2 mile (no view from here). Continue on the nearly level trail through the forest, passing a wide meadow cut by a narrow shortcut trail 0.8 mile from the junction. Continuing, you plunge into the burned area and slowly descend to the first of a series of increasingly dramatic viewpoints on the peak's south side. From the last, best, viewpoint the trail heads up, levels off, and reenters the forest; follow it, past a 0.1-mile spur to more views, to the start of the loop and back down to the trailhead.

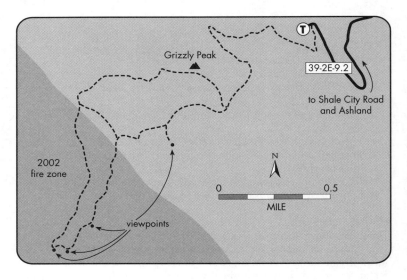

Opposite: Monkey Face, Smith Rock State Park

EAST OF THE
CASCADES

LITTLE THREE CREEK LAKE

BEFORE YOU GO
For current conditions and
more information, contact
Sisters Ranger District, *www
.fs.fed.us/r6/centraloregon* or
(541) 549-7700

ABOUT THE HIKE
Day hike or backpack
Easy to moderate for children
**3.2 round trip or 3.7-mile
loop**
190 feet elevation gain
High point 6710 feet
Hikable July through October

GETTING THERE
- From US 20/State 126 in
  Sisters, turn south on Elm
  Street (becomes Forest Road
  16/Three Creek Road)

- Drive 15.7 miles (the last 1.5 miles on very rough gravel road) to
  the road to Driftwood Campground
- Turn right and park at the trailhead near the start of the road
- Alternately, continue 0.4 mile to the end of the Driftwood
  Campground road and park at the sign to Little Three Creek
  Lake Trail

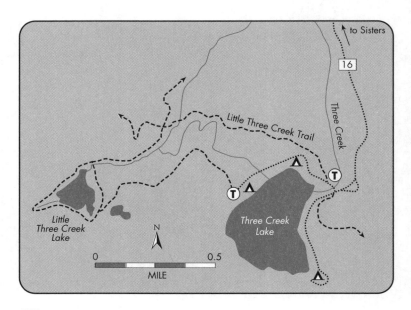

Little Three Creek Lake

HIKING THE TRAIL

A short drive from Sisters is Three Creek Lake, a good spot for primitive car camping in summer. A short hike from Three Creek Lake is Little Three Creek Lake, more remote and stunningly beautiful, with the rocky bluffs of Tam McArthur Rim as a backdrop.

Start up the hill, bearing left in a couple of minutes at the trail junction. At 0.6 cross a creek, then another, passing a boggy meadow on the left. At 1.1, bear left at the four-way trail junction. You'll meet and follow a creek as the trail ascends to reach the lake at 1.6 miles. The gravelly shoreline is not very inviting for swimming but could accommodate some feet-cooling.

Return as you came, or continue around the lake on an informal trail, bearing left where the trail seems to want to go up onto the rocks to the right, and crossing the lake's outfall at 2.5 miles. Not quite 0.2 mile farther look for a small pond off to your right (*Littler* Little Three Creek Lake?). Head toward the pond, then ease left, keeping the pond on your right, to pick up a trail leading 0.6 mile to another trailhead at the end of the Driftwood Campground road. Follow the road 0.4 mile back to your car.

 **BLACK BUTTE**

BEFORE YOU GO
For current conditions and more information, contact Sisters Ranger District, *www.fs.fed.us/r6/centraloregon* or (541) 549-7700

ABOUT THE HIKE
Day hike
Moderate to challenging for children
4 miles round trip
1640 feet elevation gain
High point 6440 feet
Hikable June through October

GETTING THERE
- From the junction of State Highway 22 and US Highway 20/State Highway 126,

drive east 20 miles on US 20/State 126 to Indian Ford Road
- Turn north and drive 0.2 mile
- Bear left onto Green Ridge Road (Forest Road 11) and drive 3.7 miles
- Turn left on gravel Forest Road 1110 and drive 5.3 miles to the trailhead parking area

HIKING THE TRAIL
Gaze at it from Black Butte Ranch resort, or drive by it on the highway, and the tall, black, symmetrical cinder cone of Black Butte just looks like something you'd want to climb. The road goes most of the way up; 2 miles of hiking finishes the ascent. On top you can visit a

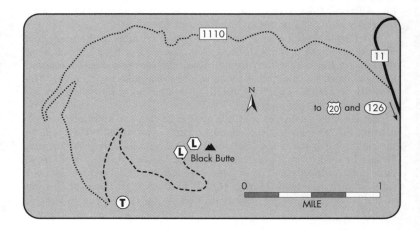

Black Butte summit

couple of lookout towers, adding to the uniqueness of this hike.

The route starts northward around the butte, ascending steadily through a forest of ponderosa pines. Small signs identify manzanita, chinkapin, snowbrush, and other understory plants at trail side. At 0.6 mile the forest's character changes suddenly and becomes cooler as you enter a grove dominated by grand fir. Round a switchback at 0.8 mile and soon the trail emerges from the trees, granting views of Mount Washington and the Three Sisters. Look for scarlet gilia, balsam root, and other wildflowers on the open slopes here in midsummer.

The view just gets better and better—of nearby mountains as well as of the manicured fairways of the resort below. Just before climbing onto the summit, the trail enters a grove of subalpine fir, then passes through an old burn, evidence of the 1981 Black Butte fire. Look east to see Smith Rock jutting from the high desert floor.

Once on top, look for the 18-foot cupola lookout tower, built in 1924. (An 83-foot tower built here in 1934 toppled in a storm in 2001.) A sign describes the development of fire lookout facilities on Black Butte, starting with an open platform constructed between two fir trees in 1910 and ending with the 1979 log cabin tucked just over the ridge near the cupola (occupied in summer, but not open to the public).

METOLIUS RIVER

BEFORE YOU GO
For current conditions and
more information, contact
Sisters Ranger District, *www
.fs.fed.us/r6/centraloregon* or
(541) 549-7700

ABOUT THE HIKE
Day hike
Easy to moderate for children
Up to 6-mile loop
150 feet elevation gain
High point 2900 feet
Hikable most of the year

GETTING THERE
- From US Highway 20, 9 miles west of Sisters, turn north at a sign for Camp Sherman (milepost 90)
- Follow signs 5 miles to Camp Sherman
- Turn left onto Forest Road 14 and drive about 5 miles
- Turn left, across the Metolius River, to Wizard Falls Fish Hatchery

HIKING THE TRAIL
Trails follow one or both sides of the scenic Metolius River from its headwaters near Camp Sherman to the end of paved road access, about 10 miles to the north. It's jammed with fly fishermen in summer; consider a visit in the quiet spring or fall. You could start a hike at any of several campgrounds strung along the river. Best of all, start at Wizard Falls Fish Hatchery. Bring quarters for the coin-operated fish food dispensers; scatter the pellets in the rearing tanks to watch the larger trout, kokanee, and Atlantic salmon lunge and strike. The biggest fish are in the big settling pond at the north end of the hatchery; one day a year (usually the second Saturday in June) kids are invited to go fishing here and to

Wizard Falls fish hatchery

keep one fish. Don't bother looking for Wizard Falls; it used to tumble into the river from a side creek, but it disappeared in 1947 when the creek's flow was diverted to the hatchery that took its name.

From the hatchery, hikers have several options. Head south on the river's west bank (opposite from the road) for a 5.7-mile out-and-back hike to the trail's end at Lower Canyon Creek Campground (or sooner). The trail climbs a bit initially, to views above where the river branches among brushy islands; watch for water ouzels and, in early summer, wildflowers. Notice the little scratches in rocks in the trail? They're from the cleats on fishermen's waders. At about 0.7 mile the trail returns to river level. The river is swift and cold (48 degrees

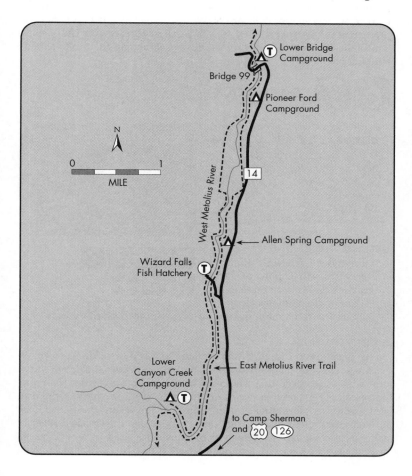

year-round), but careful toe-dipping and wading is possible in places.

Heading north from the hatchery, trails follow both sides of the river for 3 miles before reaching the road bridge at Lower Bridge Campground, allowing a 6-mile loop hike if your party can handle it. Otherwise, pick a side; the eastside trail hugs the river past Allen Spring Campground at 0.4 mile, to a fence line at 1 mile. Follow the trail east, then north again, bypassing a tract of private property and entering a cool Douglas fir forest. Pass Pioneer Ford Campground at 0.4 mile before reaching the bridge. A return on the west side of the river starts on an exposed and, in summer, hot trail but veers away from the river at 0.75 mile, passing a wetland and entering a cool forest of mixed conifers (steering clear of more private riverside property). You'll walk through a grove of incense cedars before returning to the river at 1.75 miles. Approaching the hatchery, you'll cross a small footbridge over the settling pond's discharge stream before winding back among the tanks to your starting point.

 SMITH ROCK

BEFORE YOU GO
For current conditions and more information, contact Smith Rock State Park, www.oregonstateparks.org or (541) 548-7501

ABOUT THE HIKE
Day hike
Easy to challenging for children
1.5 to 2.2 miles round trip
180 to 840 feet elevation gain
High point 3320 feet
Hikable most of the year

GETTING THERE
- From Bend, follow US Highway 97 north 22 miles at the sign to Smith Rock State Park
- Turn east and follow signs 3.2 miles to the main day-use area for Smith Rock State Park

HIKING THE TRAIL
Smith Rock draws climbers from around the world to tackle its steep, intricate pitches. Most of the cars in the parking lot seem to belong to climbers—and a few spectators who come to watch climbers spider their way up seemingly impossible routes or simply to drink in views of the dramatic ochre rock formations jutting from the high desert. But Smith Rock also offers excellent hiking, from tame paths along the Crooked River to short but taxing ascents. Plan a picnic lunch at a sandy riverside beach, or challenge the kids with a climb to Misery Ridge. In the heat of summer,

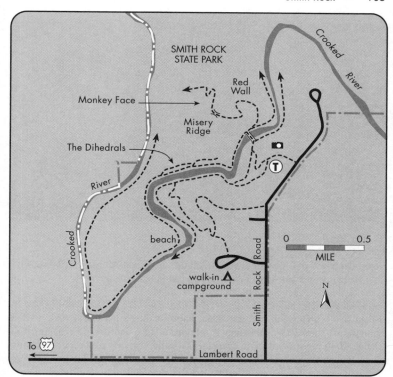

plan your visit for early or late in the day. There is no car/RV campground here, though there is a climbers' bivouac area for primitive camping. The trail network here is extensive. Following are just two of several options to consider with children.

RIVER PATH (2.2 MILES ROUND TRIP, 180 FEET ELEVATION GAIN)

From the bluff at the day-use area, asphalt paths lead to a rock-walled viewpoint, then down 180 feet in elevation to a footbridge crossing the Crooked River on either a gradual 0.3-mile trail or a steeper 0.2-mile path. From here the hike is nearly level. Cross the footbridge and turn left, with the flow of the river. At 0.3 mile from the footbridge look across the river to see Rope de Dope Rock, a favorite spot for beginning climbers. At 0.4 mile a spur route splits off uphill to the Dihedrals climbing area. A few minutes later, look up to the right to the round rock poised in Asterisk Pass. The trail narrows but continues; the sandy beach 0.9 mile from the footbridge makes a good turnaround spot. More energetic hikers could continue around to the base of the famous Monkey Face

Smith Rock

formation, even following a rough, steep path past Monkey Face to Misery Ridge. From the footbridge a trail leads upriver as well.

MISERY RIDGE (1.5 MILES ROUND TRIP, 840 FEET ELEVATION GAIN)
From the bluff at the day-use area, asphalt paths lead to a rock-walled viewpoint, then down 180 feet in elevation to a footbridge crossing the Crooked River on either a gradual 0.3-mile trail or a steeper 0.2-mile path. From the footbridge, bear right, then immediately left away from the river toward the formation called the Red Wall. The trail steadily ascends the rock on a series of steps, a rickety wooden staircase, and a footpath. Take it slow and you'll make it all the way to aptly named Misery Ridge, just 0.5 mile but 660 feet from the river. Drop-offs are steep; keep a close eye on children. Return as you came (though more experienced adventurers can manage the alternate return routes down the back side).

FUN UNDER THE SUN—SAFELY

Dermatologists now warn that sunburn on young children can be a precursor to skin cancer years later. So protecting children from sunburn in their early years does a lot to help them stay healthy as adults. Always carry and use sunscreen. Some children are allergic to PABA, the active ingredient in most sunscreens; pediatricians suggest using a non-PABA lotion with a sun protection factor (SPF) of at least 15 to 30, particularly if skin is very fair. Be sure to reapply it after a couple of hours, even if you've used a higher SPF sunscreen.

DESCHUTES RIVER SOUTH CANYON

BEFORE YOU GO
For current conditions and more information, contact Bend Metro Parks District, *www.bendparksandrec.org* or (541) 389-7275

ABOUT THE HIKE
Day hike
Easy for children
3-mile loop
Nearly level
High point 3630 feet
Hikable May through November

GETTING THERE

- From US Highway 97 in Bend (south of downtown), turn west at Reed Market Road
- Drive about 1 mile and park at Farewell Bend Park, just before the road crosses the Deschutes River

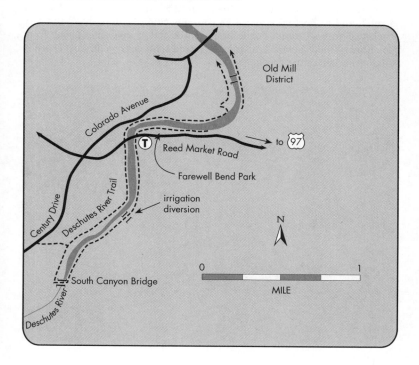

HIKING THE TRAIL

With so many wilderness trails available to choose from so close to Bend, why choose this one right in town? Sometimes you don't feel like driving even a half hour, and many of those trails are snowed in until summer. Recent extension of Bend's 11-mile Deschutes River Trail and addition of a new footbridge in the south canyon provides a bit of wildness right in town. It's not remote—you can see office buildings or houses much of the way—but it's the musical river, the mergansers and geese, and Ponderosa pines under the rimrock that you're more likely to notice. Snow can block the trail through the deep, shady canyon until mid-spring.

Start at the playground at Farewell Bend Park. For a counterclockwise hike, cross the Reed Market Road bridge on foot and start up the path on the west side of the river. The trail stays close to river level most of the way, with interpretive signs here and there. A side trail to Mount Bachelor Village Resort enters at 1.1 mile, then at 1.5 miles the trail ends (as of 2006) at a slender bridge spanning the river. Cross it and return on the other side, bearing left at trail junctions (leading to neighborhood trails). About 0.6 mile from the footbridge the trail leads onto a boardwalk at an irrigation diversion structure. After a short boggy stretch and a short rocky stretch, you're back on level path all the way back to Farewell Bend. For a longer walk, follow riverside paths from downtown Bend (about 6 miles total round trip) or the Old Mill District (about 5 miles round trip).

Farewell Bend Park

69 **TUMALO FALLS**

BEFORE YOU GO
For current conditions and more information, contact Bend/Fort Rock Ranger District, *www.fs .fed.us/r6/centraloregon* or (541) 383-4000

ABOUT THE HIKE
Day hike or backpack
Easy to challenging for children
0.4 to 2.0 miles round trip; 6.8-mile loop
Up to 1100 feet elevation gain
High point 6040 feet
Hikable June through October

GETTING THERE

- From the west side of Bend, head west on Galveston Avenue (becomes Skyliners Road)
- Drive about 10 miles to gravel Forest Road 4601

- Turn right and continue across Tumalo Creek on a single-lane bridge
- Immediately bear left onto Forest Road 4603
- Drive 3.4 miles to Tumalo Falls Picnic Area

HIKING THE TRAIL

This entire loop would challenge most children, but even brand-new hikers can handle the 0.4-mile round trip to the top of Tumalo Falls. Those with a little more ambition could take on the 2-mile, round-trip hike to Double Falls. The entire loop, passing more and wilder waterfalls and miles of forest, challenges most children, though the ascent is gradual. It's a good choice for older children who like to hike and want to stretch themselves.

Tumalo Falls, right at the trailhead, is a destination in itself: a wide cataract free-falling onto a rock staircase. Follow signs up North Fork Trail and continue straight where Bridge Creek Trail comes in on the left. At 0.2 mile, the top of the falls, pause to take in the view from a platform cantilevered out from the cliffs. The surrounding forest still bears witness to the 1979 Bridge Creek Fire, which burned 4200 acres of old-growth forest. Follow the trail along the fence to return to the main trail.

Tumalo Creek rushes below you as the trail gently ascends through the pines and firs. At 1 mile you'll see Double Falls, a series of two wide cascades spilling down basalt ledges into a green pool (steep drop-off; take care). Another 0.9 mile leads to Upper Falls, sliding over a steep dome of rock. Just 0.5 mile farther the trail crosses Tumalo Creek's Middle Fork on a narrow bridge—another possible turnaround and/or picnic spot. From here the trail steepens, and as it does, the waterfalls abound.

At 3.4 miles you'll reach the junction with Spring Creek Trail; bear left to reach the Middle Fork in another 0.3 mile.

To complete the loop, wade the creek or walk upstream a short distance to cross on a log. The trail resumes across the creek, level, then drops gently to reach a permit station (free at this writing) at the entrance to the City of Bend watershed not quite a mile from the creek crossing. Continue dropping through forest, crossing Spring Creek, and hiking 1 mile more to the junction with Bridge Creek Trail. At the junction turn left and follow Bridge Creek Trail 1.3 miles alongside stair-stepping Bridge Creek to the junction with the Tumalo Creek Trail just above the parking area.

Tumalo Falls

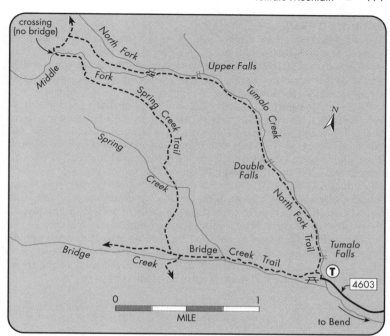

crossing
(no bridge)

North Fork

Middle

Fork

Spring Creek Trail

Upper Falls

Tumalo Creek

Spring

Creek

Double
Falls

North Fork Trail

Bridge

Creek

Bridge Creek Trail

Tumalo
Falls

T

4603

0   1

MILE

to Bend

 TUMALO MOUNTAIN

BEFORE YOU GO
For current conditions and more information, contact Bend/Fort Rock Ranger District, *www .fs.fed.us/r6/centraloregon* or (541) 383-4000

ABOUT THE HIKE
Day hike
Challenging for children
4 miles round trip
1415 feet elevation gain
High point 7775 feet
Hikable July through October

GETTING THERE

- From Bend, head south and west on Century Drive (becomes Cascade Lakes Highway and Forest Road 46)
- Drive about 25 miles
- Turn right into the Tumalo Mountain trailhead (also a winter snow-park area)
- This trailhead is just past the first Mount Bachelor turnoff and 3 miles west of the Sunriver cutoff road

HIKING THE TRAIL

What's it like to climb a mountain? Like a very long hike that gets steeper and steeper. The steeper it gets, the slower you go, and the last half-mile can feel like 10 miles. But when you get to the top you feel like you're at the top of the world, and if you've paced yourself right, you're tired—a really good kind of tired.

Tumalo Mountain can give children a taste of that experience in a relatively short outing. The hike begins as a gradual but steady ascent through a forest, then breaks into the open, and steepens radically for the final ascent. At the top, you're clearly not on top of the world: Mount Bachelor is close enough that you'll feel you could hit it with a well-aimed rock, but it's 1290 feet higher. At the top of Tumalo, however, the panorama is grand, with views of Broken Top's crater, the Three Sisters, Sparks Lake, the verdant Tumalo Creek drainage, Bend, and even Smith Rock in the distance. It can be chilly and windy at the top, so carry an extra shirt or windbreaker for lingering on the summit.

The trail begins at the east end of the parking area and winds uphill, alternating between forest and meadow. Peek through the trees to see the ski runs on Mount Bachelor. Note how contorted some of the trees are, a result of being under snow more than half the year.

Three Sisters and Broken Top from Tumalo Mountain

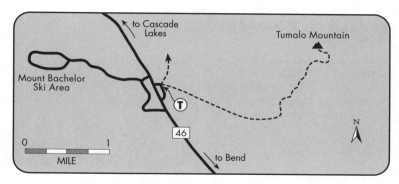

For the final 0.5 mile the forest falls away and you walk straight up the steep trail to the summit. This is a good place to teach children the "wedding march" style of hiking, emulating climbers, as an alternative to the hike-rest-hike-rest style that kids can fall into. When you do stop to rest, kids who ski in winter will enjoy seeing Mount Bachelor's snow-free runs so clearly etched among the trees. On the return hike, they may wish they had ski poles to help them schuss down the steep summit trail.

YOU ARE WHAT YOU DRINK: WATER

Our bodies are made mostly of water—about 50 to 60 percent for most of us. The fitter you are, the more water in your body; adult athletes are close to 70 percent water. The more active you are, the more you sweat, the more water you need to drink to replace the water you're losing. Hiking in hot weather puts you at risk of heat exhaustion, but it's easy to prevent. You get it by not taking in as much liquid as you are eliminating, and you prevent it by drinking more water than you may think you need. Everyone, no matter how young, should always carry his or her own water bottle.

The early symptoms of heat exhaustion are deceptively like flu: muscle cramps, fatigue, weakness, sweating, sometimes nausea. Don't expect hot skin; people with heat exhaustion are more likely to have cool, clammy skin and a normal or slightly depressed temperature. If you suspect heat exhaustion in someone, get him to lie down in a cool, comfortable place and start sipping, then drinking, fluids—salty fluids if you have them, but anything will help. You should notice rapid improvement.

TODD LAKE

BEFORE YOU GO
For current conditions and more information, contact Bend/Fort Rock Ranger District, *www .fs.fed.us/r6/centraloregon* or (541) 383-4000

ABOUT THE HIKE
Day hike
Easy for children
2.4-mile loop
Nearly level
High point 6150 feet
Hikable July through October

GETTING THERE

- From Bend, head south and west on Century Drive (becomes Cascade Lakes Highway and Forest Road 46)
- Drive about 26 miles (1.5 miles past Mount Bachelor) to a sign to Todd Lake
- Turn right and drive 0.5 mile to the parking area above the meadow

HIKING THE TRAIL
The southern end of picturesque, 45-acre Todd Lake is just 0.2 mile from the trailhead parking area, making it a popular spot for camping on late-summer weekends. That accessibility also makes it appealing for an easy, level hike. Count on mosquitoes early in the season; all season wear boots (or expect soggy sneakers) for walking around the lake's marshy far end.

Begin hiking up the gated road marked with a campground sign.

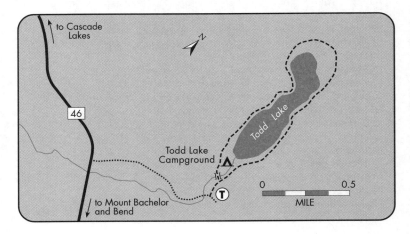

A short distance from the parking area the road splits; you can go in either direction to circle Todd Lake. Going clockwise, cross the lake's outlet to reach a small campground on the lakeshore; Broken Top can be seen rising beyond the water. Walk to the lake edge and pick up the trail, which closely follows the shore.

Wildflowers border the trail here and there; occasionally you'll step over wet spots where springs are seeping into the lake. Approaching the lake's far end, cross rivulets that zigzag across a widening meadow. The trail per se disappears at the far end, where the terrain gets soggy. Pick a route to stay as dry as possible.

Pick up the trail where the marsh gives way to drier ground. The trail then reenters the forest, following close to the lake's east shore for the walk back to the junction.

Todd Lake

 LAVA RIVER CAVE

BEFORE YOU GO
For current conditions and more information, contact Bend/Fort Rock Ranger District, www.fs.fed.us/r6/centraloregon or (541) 383-4000, or Lava Lands Visitor Center, (541) 593-2421 (April through October)

ABOUT THE HIKE
Day hike
Easy for children
2.4 miles round trip
200 feet elevation gain
High point 4500 feet
Hikable early May through mid-October

GETTING THERE

- From Bend take US Highway 97 south about 14 miles
- Turn east at the sign to Lava River Cave

HIKING THE TRAIL

Hiking in a cave? It's quite possible—and enticing to children—when the cave is a mile-long uncollapsed lava tube. The cave is part of Newberry National Volcanic Monument. The Forest Service opens the cave to visitors late spring through mid-October, charging a small fee for admission (children under 12 free) and another nominal fee for lantern rental. Take a flashlight for back-up light, but rent a lantern as well; you can see much more than with a flashlight, and responsible children can take turns holding the light. Be sure to wear warm clothes as well; regardless of the temperature outside, the cave is always about 40 degrees Fahrenheit.

Children will be awed by the whole experience: the darkness broken by the lanterns' light and the long shadows they cast, the eerie sounds of hissing lanterns and echoing voices, and just the knowledge that they're under the earth, out of touch with familiar landmarks. Some young children may find it too frightening. Adventurous types may need reminders not to wander too far from the light; it's easy to twist an ankle wandering alone in the dark. Rest assured there are no side chambers to mistakenly wander into.

Pick up a free trail brochure at the entrance booth for interpretation along the way or for reading after the hike.

You enter the lava tube at a point where the roof collapsed thousands of years ago. Look back to see that the tube actually continues in the other direction (but is currently blocked off). Stairs lead down into the cave; once on the cave floor, begin a slow descent on a rock and sand surface with a few stairs here and there. About 0.25 mile from the entrance, the lava tube crosses under the highway (don't bother listening for cars; they're a good 80 feet above you). Then at about 0.6 mile look for the Sand Garden, where dripping water has created a fantastical landscape in a field of sand that, over centuries, has slowly entered the cave. The hike through the tube ends after 1.2 miles, where sand blocks further progress.

Extend your outing with a stop at the High Desert Museum, about 5 miles north of Lava River Cave, or at Lava Lands Visitor Center, 1 mile north of Lava River Cave. Learn about the area's volcanic history and get information about the 0.9-mile paved loop trail at Lava Cast Forest and other Newberry National Volcanic Monument points of interest.

Volcanic rock

PAULINA CREEK FALLS

BEFORE YOU GO
For current conditions and more information, contact Bend/Fort Rock Ranger District, www .fs.fed.us/r6/centraloregon or (541) 383-4000, or Lava Lands Visitor Center, (541) 593-2421 (April through October)

ABOUT THE HIKE
Day hike
Easy for children
0.4 to 0.6 mile round trip
Up to 300 feet elevation gain
High point 6330 feet
Hikable June through October

GETTING THERE
- From Bend, take US Highway 97 about 20 miles south
- Turn left at the sign to Newberry Caldera (Forest Road 21)
- Drive 12.2 miles
- Turn left into the signed parking area
- To reach the upper trailhead, continue 0.3 mile to Paulina Lake Lodge
- Park in the wide parking area south of the boat dock or in a picnic area a short distance farther on Forest Road 21

HIKING THE TRAIL
Paulina Creek tumbles down from Paulina Lake, inside Newberry Caldera. It has waterfalls at several points, though not all are easy to find from 8.5-mile Peter Skene Ogden Trail that runs parallel to the creek. This uppermost falls, 100-foot Paulina Creek Falls, is the tallest and the easiest to find and requires the shortest hike. It's a cool retreat on a hot summer's day. Or try it in late spring, when the waterfalls are gushing, or autumn, when aspen leaves flutter gold against the red ponderosa pines.

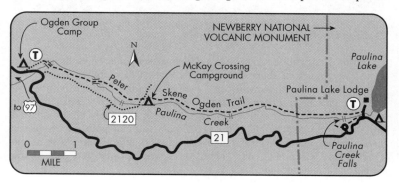

Paulina Creek

From the trailhead at the falls parking area, bear right to the main falls viewpoint in a short distance, or bear left to switchback down 0.2 mile to a viewing platform at the base of the falls. Alternatively, drive 0.3 mile farther and turn left toward Paulina Lake Lodge, parking near the lake's outlet (the start of Paulina Creek). A woodsy trail leads 0.3 mile down the south side of the creek past the viewpoint to the picnic area parking lot. Or, from the lake, cross the creek and take Peter Skene Ogden Trail down the north side of the creek 0.3 mile to a view of the falls from the other side.

For a longer hike, venture farther down Peter Skene Ogden Trail, which is rather steep at its upper end. Alternately, consider a hike up the trail from the lower trailhead at Ogden Group Camp (off Forest Road 21 just 3 miles east of US 97). After crossing a sturdy pole footbridge, it's a gentle ascent to a second footbridge at 0.9 mile. The creek here is fairly shallow and safe; it's a good spot to picnic or dip toes.

 PAULINA LAKE

BEFORE YOU GO
For current conditions and more information, contact Bend/Fort Rock Ranger District, www.fs.fed.us/r6/centraloregon or (541) 383-4000, or Lava Lands Visitor Center, (541) 593-2421 (April through October)

ABOUT THE HIKE
Day hike or backpack
Easy to challenging for children
2.5 miles round trip to 7.5-mile loop
Up to 195 feet elevation gain
High point 6330 feet
Hikable June through October

GETTING THERE
- From Bend, take US Highway 97 about 20 miles south
- Turn left at the sign to Newberry Caldera (Forest Road 21) and drive 12.5 miles
- Turn left toward Paulina Lake Campground
- Park at the boat dock past the campground

HIKING THE TRAIL
Why walk around a lake that's accessible by car? In the case of Paulina Lake, three reasons come to mind: to get to some otherwise inaccessible parts of the shoreline, to see the lake and surrounding country from a different perspective, and, perhaps most of all, to get the sense of accomplishment that accompanies such a trek. Though motorboats slowly trolling on the lake keep you from feeling "away from it all," the lake attracts more anglers than hikers, and you're likely to be alone on much of the trail. This hike is recommended for older children who enjoy a challenge. For a shorter, one-way hike (4 miles), leave a shuttle car at Little Crater Campground. For an even shorter hike, just walk down to the beach and back.

To walk clockwise, head toward Paulina Lake Lodge along the shore to a trail sign and the beginning of a footpath. The trail reaches a nice gravel beach and campsite (with outhouse) and view of Paulina Peak at about 1.25 miles. At 2 miles the trail leads away from the lake and up the hill (the only significant ascent on the trail) to avoid a steep, red rockslide along the lake.

Back down near lake level, notice the way the trail sparkles with tiny chips of obsidian; they're from an obsidian flow a few minutes ahead on the trail. The shoreline grows rockier here, more dramatic, on the approach to Little Crater Campground, at 4 miles.

Walk through the campground on the road for about 0.5 mile until the trail resumes along the now sandy lakeshore. Pass in front of some privately owned summer homes and into a wide, grassy marsh teeming with butterflies and dragonflies. The trail re-enters forest, crosses creeks on little footbridges, and emerges at Paulina Lake Campground.

BLACK GLASS AND ARROWHEADS: OBSIDIAN

Obsidian looks like what it is: black glass. It is formed when a type of volcanic lava comes in contact with water. What geologists call the Big Obsidian Flow came from the caldera between Paulina and East Lakes in Newberry Volcano (site of Hikes 73 and 74) about 1300 years ago, making it Central Oregon's most recent volcanic eruption. The rock under the caldera was rich in silica, the main ingredient in glass; when it melted from the heat of the earth, and later cooled, obsidian was formed. The First Peoples to live in this area discovered how useful obsidian is for making cutting tools, from knives to arrowheads. When it is fractured, the edges can be sharper than the finest steel blades. Tempting as it may be, don't pocket any obsidian souvenirs you find on a hike. It leaves less for others to enjoy (and it's against the law).

Paulina Lake

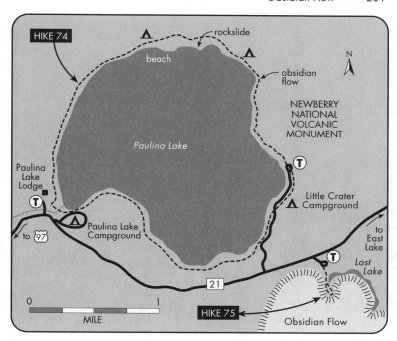

HIKE 74

rockslide

beach

obsidian flow

N

NEWBERRY NATIONAL VOLCANIC MONUMENT

Paulina Lake

Paulina Lake Lodge

T

T

Paulina Lake Campground

to ⑨⑦

Little Crater Campground

to East Lake

Lost Lake

T

21

HIKE 75

Obsidian Flow

0   1

MILE

7 5 OBSIDIAN FLOW

BEFORE YOU GO
For current conditions and more information, contact Bend/Fort Rock Ranger District, *www.fs.fed.us/r6 /centraloregon* or (541) 383-4000, or Lava Lands Visitor Center, (541) 593-2421 (April through October)

ABOUT THE HIKE
Day hike
Easy for children
0.7-mile loop
100 feet elevation gain
High point 6600 feet
Hikable June through October

GETTING THERE
- From Bend, take US Highway 97 about 20 miles south
- Turn left at the sign to Newberry Caldera (Forest Road 21)
- Drive 12.5 miles to the caldera rim
- Continue on the main road 2.3 miles to the sign for Obsidian Flow

Obsidian Flow

HIKING THE TRAIL

Though this trail is too short to qualify as a genuine hike—it's really a little interpretive trail—make a point of walking it on a visit to Newberry Caldera. Even in the volcanic Oregon Cascades, it's unlikely you'll see another mountain of black, glasslike obsidian. It's fascinating, and it offers an opportunity to talk about how glass is made from silica—a process similar to the way this obsidian was made deep inside the now-dormant Newberry Volcano. A paved trail leads safely up onto the flow. Keep the kids on the trail; off-trail, the obsidian is literally as slick and sharp as glass.

The path threads among lodgepole pines to a staircase that leads up and onto the obsidian flow; look over your left shoulder to see aptly named Lost Lake. Cross a chasm on a sturdy footbridge, then turn right or left to make the loop. Short spur trails lead to benches and viewpoints. From the highest point there's a magnificent view not only of the obsidian flow surrounding you but also of Paulina Peak, Paulina Lake, and Mt. Bachelor, South Sister, and the tip of Middle Sister.

Opposite: Beach at Ecola State Park

THE COAST AND WEST SLOPE COAST RANGE

76 CATHEDRAL TREE

BEFORE YOU GO
For more information, contact Astoria and Warrenton Area Chamber of Commerce, *www.oldoregon.com* or (800) 875-6807

ABOUT THE HIKE
Day hike
Easy for children
1 to 3 miles round trip
250 to 370 feet elevation gain
High point 595 feet
Hikable year-round

GETTING THERE

- From Marine Drive in downtown Astoria, turn up the hill at Sixteenth Street
- Turn left on Irving Avenue
- Continue to Twenty-eighth Street
- Park along the street
- To reach the Astoria Column from Sixteenth Street, turn right on Irving, left on Fifteenth Street, and follow signs to the top of Coxcomb Hill

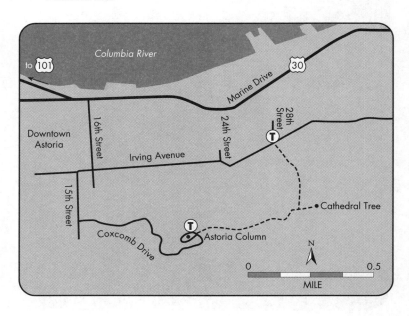

HIKING THE TRAIL

You know from its name that the Cathedral Tree is something special. This Sitka spruce is more than 300 years old, it stretches at least 200 feet to the sky, and it is 8.5 feet in diameter. It's just 1 mile from the main trailhead to the Cathedral Tree and back. Add a woodsy walk to the Astoria Column for a longer outing.

From the main trailhead, start up the wide gravel path and plunge immediately into a beautiful old forest. At 0.4 mile you'll reach a boardwalk structure with a junction in the middle. A right turn leads to the Astoria Column. Turn left to reach the Cathedral Tree in a couple of minutes. It stands in a dense, dark, cool forest on spindly "legs"

Trail to Astoria Column from Cathedral Tree

creating a kind of cave, or cathedral, at the base and indicating that it started life growing on a nurse log. It's boggy at the base, with bright yellow skunk cabbage blooming in early spring, but a boardwalk will keep your feet dry.

Head back to the boardwalk junction and make a steady, gentle ascent through the forest on a narrower trail (muddy at times). Approaching the top of the hill, ignore the trails that branch off and stick to the main trail, which emerges from the forest at the top of Coxcomb Hill, site of the Astoria Column. Built in 1926, the Column is covered with spiraling images depicting Captain Robert Gray's first glimpse of the Columbia River in 1792, the establishment of American claims to the Northwest Territory, and other key events in the history of the American West. Climb up the one hundred sixty-four steps inside (adding 125 feet of elevation gain to the hike) to a magnificent view from the little catwalk at the top. If the gift shop below is open, buy a little balsa wood airplane to fly off the top and watch it glide and land. Return as you came (or make a one-way hike with shuttle car).

THE SWEET-SMELLING SKUNK CABBAGE

You are sure to see bright yellow skunk cabbage blossoms whenever you hike past boggy areas in the coastal forest in spring. They're known for their big leaves (up to five feet long!), their tall pokerlike flower stem and, especially, their rank odor. But get down on your hands and knees and get close to the flower stem; you'll find it's really hundreds of sweet-smelling little greenish flowers under a yellow hood. That skunk smell? It's from the leaves.

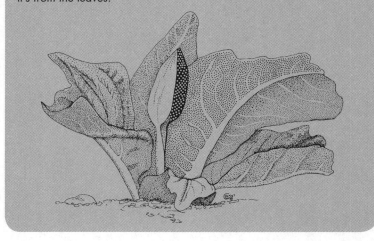

 **TILLAMOOK HEAD**

BEFORE YOU GO
For current conditions and more information, contact Ecola State Park, *www.oregonstateparks .org* or (800) 551-6949

ABOUT THE HIKE
Day hike or backpack
Moderate to challenging for children
3.2-mile or more loop; 6 miles one way
700 feet elevation gain
High point 750 feet
Hikable year-round

GETTING THERE
- From the Seaside junction of US Highways 26 and 101, take US 101 south 3 miles
- Take the first Cannon Beach exit
- Follow the road down the hill and turn right at the sign to Ecola State Park
- Follow park signs 3.7 miles to the road's end at Indian Beach

HIKING THE TRAIL
When you climb up Tillamook Head, you're walking in the footsteps of the Lewis and Clark Expedition. In January 1806, during the winter they spent at Fort Clatsop (near present-day Warrenton), several members of the "Corps of Discovery" walked over Tillamook Head to the mouth of Ecola Creek (site of Cannon Beach) after hearing reports of a beached whale. They were hoping to get some whale meat. What they got more of was what you'll get a lot of: amazing views. Crossing through magnificent old forest, you'll get glimpses of the ocean falling away below and—new since Lewis and Clark's day—Tillamook Rock Lighthouse off the headland.

Indian Beach from Tillamook Head

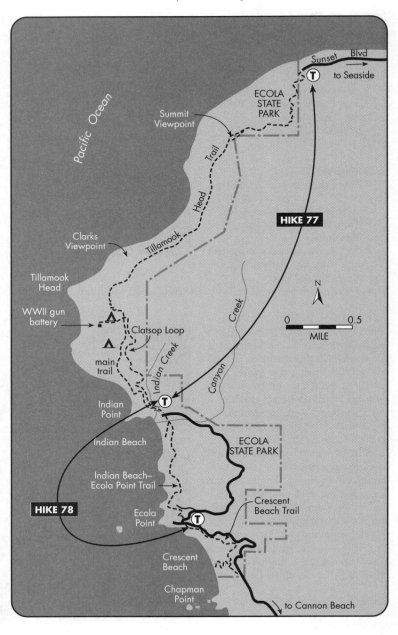

Pacific Ocean

Sunset Blvd

to Seaside

ECOLA STATE PARK

Summit Viewpoint

HIKE 77

Clarks Viewpoint

Tillamook Head Trail

Tillamook Head

WWII gun battery

Clatsop Loop

main trail

Indian Creek

Canyon Creek

Indian Point

Indian Beach

N

0   0.5
MILE

Indian Beach–Ecola Point Trail

ECOLA STATE PARK

Crescent Beach Trail

HIKE 78

Ecola Point

Crescent Beach

Chapman Point

to Cannon Beach

From parking at Indian Beach, head north to the trailhead, cross Indian Creek, and immediately bear left for a clockwise walk on Clatsop Loop. It's a fairly steady uphill climb nearly all the way; look around for nurse logs and for big stumps, left over from old logging operations. The trail tops out and drops shortly before reaching a junction at 1.4 miles. A right here returns you to the parking area via an old road alongside the creek. But continue a short distance to reach a backpackers' campsite, with three-sided shelters and a fire ring, at 1.6 miles. A road leads west 0.2 mile to the ruins of a World War II gun battery, nearly obscured by vegetation. It was built as part of a series of coastal defense fortifications. Extend your hike a bit more by walking north through deep forest a fairly level 0.7 mile to Clarks Viewpoint.

With a shuttle car you could continue north 3.7 more miles to the trail's end above the beach near Seaside. Otherwise, return to the trail junction and go left to loop back 1.3 miles on the Clatsop Loop.

 INDIAN BEACH TO ECOLA POINT

BEFORE YOU GO
For current conditions and more information, contact Ecola State Park, *www.oregonstateparks.org* or (800) 551-6949

ABOUT THE HIKE
Day hike
Moderate for children
3 miles round trip
140 feet elevation gain
High point 190 feet
Hikable year-round

GETTING THERE
- From the Seaside junction of US Highways 26 and 101, take US 101 south 3 miles

- Take the first Cannon Beach exit
- Follow the road down the hill and turn right at the sign to Ecola State Park
- Follow park signs 2 miles to parking at Ecola Point, where the trail ends
- Drive 1.7 miles farther to the trailhead at Indian Beach

HIKING THE TRAIL
The path between Ecola and Indian Points leads above a rocky and dramatic stretch of coastline accessible only to hikers. It's a fun, easy hike— one way, or round trip—for families vacationing in Cannon Beach.

For a north-to-south hike (putting the wind at your back in summer), start at Indian Beach parking lot and follow the sign to the ocean beach. Cross Canyon Creek, then bear left at the fork, rather than right to the

Stormy day at Ecola State Park

beach. The trail alternates between woodsy path and shoreline vista trail as it gradually ascends along the bluff above the sea. At about 0.5 mile the trail reaches a rather steep slide area. At 0.8 mile the trail crosses an open slope with flowers in the spring, a good spot to rest and watch for fishing boats in summer. The trail emerges from the woods at the edge of the Ecola Point parking area at 1.5 miles. Get a ride back or return as you came.

Extend your outing with a 1.2-mile hike from Ecola Point to hidden Crescent Beach. Pick up the trail at the southeast corner of the parking lot, near the rest rooms. After climbing some stairs you'll reach the park road; follow it for a few paces until the trail resumes, heading down the bank to the west. It rolls through ancient forest (muddy in places), crossing a creek on a footbridge at about 0.5 mile. At 1 mile you'll reach a junction. Here you will turn right, switchback down the steep hillside, cross another little bridge, and come to the beach. Return as you came (250 feet total elevation gain).

 WILSON RIVER TRAIL

BEFORE YOU GO
For current conditions and more information, contact Tillamook State Forest, *www.oregon.gov/odf* or (503) 842-2545, or Tillamook Forest Center, *www.tillamookforest.org* or (503) 359-7439

ABOUT THE HIKE
Day hike
Easy to moderate for children
2 miles round trip or 4 miles one way
Rolling
High point 600 feet
Hikable most of the year

GETTING THERE
- From Portland, take US Highway 26 northwest about

22 miles to the exit for State Highway 6
- Follow State 6 southwest 20 miles to Tillamook Forest Center at milepost 22
- Jones Creek Trailhead is just off State 6 west of milepost 23
- To reach the footbridge at the hike's west end, continue west on State 6
- Turn right at the wayside just west of milepost 20

HIKING THE TRAIL

A series of massive forest fires devastated this part of the Coast Range in the 1930s and 1940s—hard to imagine when you drive through the lush (and well-logged) forest here today. Forest recovery and eventual resumption of logging have been the management focus of Tillamook State Forest for most of the past half-century, but a new focus on recreation has resulted in a spreading network of trails—a boon to Portland families, who can get here in less than an hour. Coast Range winter rains are legendary, but the trails are snow-free most of the year. Look for delicate pink fawn lilies blooming in April.

Start this hike at the broad pedestrian bridge crossing the Wilson River at the Tillamook Forest Center, which opened in 2006. Inside are lots of hands-on exhibits exploring the human and natural history of the surrounding forest; outside are nature trails, an antique "steam donkey" once used for logging, and a replica of a 1950s-style

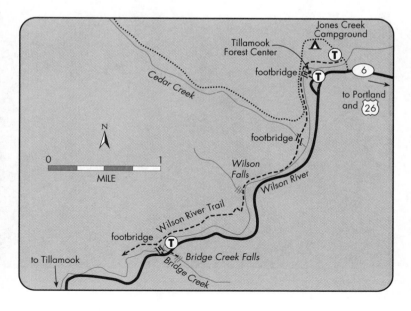

fire lookout tower you can visit. The bridge leads directly out from the exhibit area, crosses the river, and intersects the Wilson River Trail (which extends for several miles in both directions). If the center is closed, start your hike just upstream at Jones Creek Trailhead and walk west (downstream) about 0.5 mile to the new footbridge.

From the interpretive center bridge, it's a gentle 1 mile of walking to reach the little log footbridge at Cedar Creek, a good turnaround or picturesque picnic spot. Continuing, the trail stays close to the river, crossing a side creek at Wilson Falls at about 2 miles, and reaches a spur trail to the lower footbridge at 3.8 miles. Take the spur trail a short distance, into and out of a dry side channel of the river, to the footbridge that leads back across the Wilson River. Leave a shuttle car at the wayside just east of here for a one-way hike, but use extreme **caution** walking along the highway shoulder from the footbridge to the wayside.

With great care, you could extend your outing with a visit to 40-foot Bridge Creek Falls. Across the highway from the lower footbridge, look for stone steps leading off the road; they signal the start of a 0.1-mile trail to the falls. It must date from an era when the road was not as busy, nor the traffic as fast.

Wilson River Trail

FROM TILLAMOOK BURN TO TILLAMOOK FOREST

From 1933 to 1951 a series of devastating wildfires struck Oregon's northern Coast Range every six years. The fires burned some 550 square miles of forest. With habitat lost, wildlife dwindled. Rivers became choked with sediment and debris. Then a huge replanting effort began. Using helicopters, professional tree planters, and hundreds of volunteers, including many schoolchildren, 72 million tree seedlings were planted. Those trees have grown so tall that it's now hard to see evidence of the fire. What was called the Tillamook Burn for generations became, in 1973, Tillamook State Forest. Logging has resumed and, with it, debate over how best to balance the need for lumber and jobs with the need to protect watersheds and forest habitat.

 UNIVERSITY FALLS

BEFORE YOU GO
For current conditions and more information, contact Tillamook State Forest, *www.oregon.gov /odf* or (503) 842-2545

ABOUT THE HIKE
Day hike
Easy for children
0.6 mile round trip
Slight ascent and level
High point 1300 feet
Hikable most of the year

GETTING THERE
- From Portland, take US Highway 26 northwest about 22 miles to the exit for State Highway 6
- Follow State 6 southwest 9 miles and turn left at the sign to Rogers Camp Trailhead, just west of milepost 33
- Stay on the main road for 3.6 miles
- Park at the small trailhead turnout on the right

HIKING THE TRAIL
University Falls is the best-known waterfall in the Coast Range. It curtains 55 feet down a tiered rock cliff face and is especially impressive in spring (it's down to a few horsetails of water in late summer). The trails around the falls are popular with bikers, so they're rather rutted, making the hike a bumpy slog in wet weather, but the falls are a fine reward. Consider a visit to Tillamook Forest Center as well (see Hike 79).

Take the trail north out of the trailhead. It ascends, crosses a rutted road, immediately crosses another dirt road, then descends to a flat, wide area. From here a narrower trail leads left to the base of the falls in a minute or two. Return as you came.

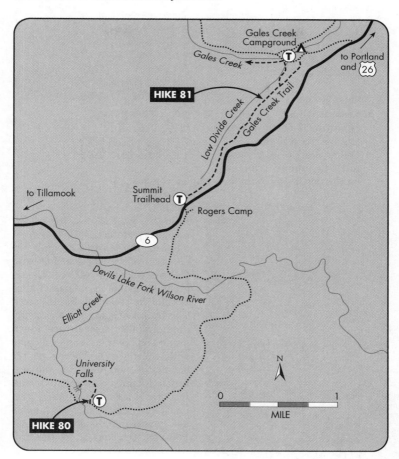

Opposite: University Falls

GALES CREEK TRAIL

BEFORE YOU GO
For current conditions and more information, contact Tillamook State Forest, *www.oregon.gov /odf* or (503) 842-2545

ABOUT THE HIKE
Day hike
Easy to moderate for children
2 miles one way
630 feet elevation loss
High point 1580 feet
Hikable most of the year

GETTING THERE
- From Portland, take US Highway 26 northwest to the exit for State Highway 6
- Follow State 6 southwest 9 miles to Summit Trailhead, on the north side of the highway at milepost 33

HIKING THE TRAIL
From the west, Gales Creek Trail actually starts on Low Divide Creek, following the musical stream's verdant canyon to its meeting with Gales Creek at Gales Creek Campground, east of the Coast Range summit in Tillamook State Forest. The trail continues, but the campground makes a good turnaround (or an end point for a one-way hike with shuttle car). There's no big destination on this trail—no waterfall to find, no summit vistas. It's simply a beautiful, mossy glen and a fairly easy trail that's hikable nearly year-round and very close to Portland. You may share the trail with mountain bikers.

From Summit Trailhead, the trail plunges down 0.25 mile to the canyon floor, then rolls along the burbling creek's south bank through a carpet of ferns and a

Gales Creek Trail

forest of moss-covered alders. The trail is technically closed to mountain bikers, and while you may find wheel ruts, they're not as bad as on some other trails in the forest. At 1.6 miles the trail crosses a side creek, then switchbacks up the hill once. Approaching the Gales Creek Campground, the trail rises to a junction; the lefthand fork takes you closer to the campground, while the right fork ends at the campground road in 2 miles.

You could make a one-way hike, or begin your hike at the campground, in summer, when the campground and its access road are open. Look for it just west of milepost 35. There are no services at the Summit Trailhead; drive west 10 miles to Smith Homestead Day-Use Area for toilets and picnic tables. Or continue west 10 miles to visit the Tillamook Forest Interpretive Center (see Hike 79).

CAPE FALCON

BEFORE YOU GO
For current conditions and more information, contact Oswald West State Park, *www.oregonstateparks.org* or (800) 551-6949

ABOUT THE HIKE
Day hike
Moderate for children
5 miles round trip
300 feet elevation gain
High point 240 feet
Hikable year-round

GETTING THERE
- From Cannon Beach, take US Highway 101 south 10 miles
- Turn right into the first (the northernmost) of three parking areas for Oswald West State Park

HIKING THE TRAIL
The hike out to Cape Falcon leads through a wonderful coastal forest with all its delights: birds twittering, shafts of sunlight playing through the lacy conifer branches, and trickling creeks. At the end, follow a narrow corridor onto the grassy, brushy, but treeless cape, where children can follow mazes in the salal and watch for whales and fishing boats offshore.

You could actually begin at any of the parking areas; a maze of loop trails winds through the forest here. The simplest approach is to pick up the trail leading west from the northernmost parking lot. The trail winds through an inspiring forest above Short Sand Creek, roaring to its meeting with the Pacific. At about 0.5 mile turn right at the trail junction. Soon the trail crosses a small creek and, at 1 mile, enters an

Neahkahnie Mountain from Cape Falcon Trail

old logged-off blowdown area. Just past the blowdown area, you will see—still standing—the kinds of trees that blew down: huge spruce, hemlock, and Douglas fir.

The trail continues to roll along, crossing small creeks. On a sunny day you will see the ocean sparkling through the trees. At about 1.8 miles the trail enters a clearing, granting views south to Short Sand Beach and Neahkahnie Mountain. At 2 miles, after a climb up a couple of short switchbacks, there's an even better view. Continue following the contours of the hill on the mostly level path to a junction, unsigned, with a spur trail leading west onto the top of Cape Falcon. Follow it 0.2 mile, through a virtual tunnel of salal at first, onto the treeless, wind-swept cape tip—a dramatic spot. It's not particularly hazardous as long as children use reasonable care, but the cliffs are steep. Return as you came. The trail, part of the long-distance Oregon Coast Trail, continues north to Arch Cape.

Extend your outing with a visit to Short Sand Beach, following signs south and west about 0.5 mile from your parking spot at Oswald West State Park. Wade in the waves, dig in the sand, picnic, or watch the surfers.

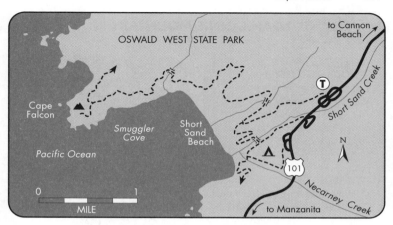

FOR CLOTHES, CANOES, AND CURES: SITKA SPRUCE

Sitka spruce dominate the forests of the coastal fog zone, sometimes mingling with Douglas fir. The largest are generally 8 to 12 feet in diameter and four hundred to seven hundred years old. You can visit the world's tallest Sitka spruce a few miles inland from US 101 on US 26 near Seaside; it measures 16.5 feet in diameter and 216 feet tall at the point where the top has broken off. Coastal natives wove spruce's long, sinewy roots into baskets, rain hats, and ropes for whaling, used its pitch to caulk whaling canoes, and brewed its inner bark into a tea to soothe sore throats. Its strong, resilient, lightweight wood was used to build airplanes during World War I. Identify them by their cones, scattered on the ground; they're 3 to 4 inches long, like Douglas fir cones, but lighter in color, with thin, papery scales and without bracts sticking out between the scales.

NEAHKAHNIE MOUNTAIN

BEFORE YOU GO
For current conditions and more information, contact Oswald West State Park, *www.oregonstateparks.org* or (800) 551-6949

ABOUT THE HIKE
Day hike
Moderate to challenging for children
3 miles round trip
890 feet elevation gain
High point 1631 feet
Hikable year-round

GETTING THERE

- From Manzanita, drive north on US Highway 101 for 1.5 miles to a hiker sign
- Turn east on a rough gravel access road
- Drive 0.5 mile to the trailhead
- Alternately, drive south about 13 miles from Cannon Beach to the access road

HIKING THE TRAIL

Legend has it that somewhere on Neahkahnie Mountain a treasure trove two-hundred-plus years old lies buried, waiting to be discovered. Whether or not it's true, it's a great source of speculation on a trek to the summit of this looming north coast landmark. The easiest way up is from the south, though a trail leads to the summit from the northwest as well. The trail ascends steadily, switchbacking up the hillside in and out of gloomy Sitka spruce stands and open hillsides thick with salal and salmonberry or, in

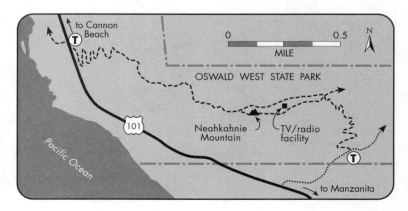

spring, such wildflowers as the pink coast fawn lily. The fourth switch-back (0.5 mile from the trailhead) offers the first of many great views. Kids may see landmarks they recognize, including US 101, the Nehalem River and Bay, and the towns of Nehalem and Wheeler.

Continue climbing the mountain's south side, up more than a dozen switchbacks, to a wooden trail marker post at the summit ridge (1.2 miles). Bear left up the forest road to a collection of radio and TV anten-nas at a cement-block building. Round the building on a rough trail and

Sitka spruce tunnel on Neahkahnie Mountain Trail

continue a few steps through the woods to the tiny, knobby summit. It's a great perch for a picnic on a sunny day. Children must take care in climbing around the steep hillside. Return as you came.

With a shuttle car you have another option. You can continue west and north down the mountain through 4.5 miles of gorgeous forest to the mountain's northern trailhead, on US 101 about 1.5 miles north of where the southern trailhead access road leaves the highway (and about 1 mile south of the southernmost parking area at Oswald West State Park).

 CAPE LOOKOUT

BEFORE YOU GO
For current conditions and more information, contact Cape Lookout State Park, *www.oregonstateparks.org* or (800) 551-6949

ABOUT THE HIKE
Day hike
Moderate for children
5 miles round trip
500 feet elevation gain
High point 850 feet
Hikable year-round

GETTING THERE
- From Tillamook, follow signs west and south about 10 miles to the entrance to Cape Lookout State Park and campground
- Continue on Cape Lookout Road 2.8 miles more
- Park at the trailhead parking area on the right
- Alternately, from Pacific City follow Three Capes Scenic Route north 13 miles to the trailhead

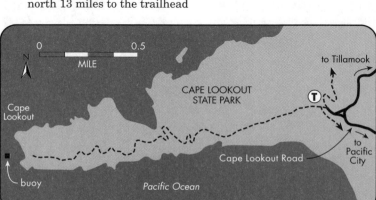

Cape Lookout

HIKING THE TRAIL

The great appeal of a hike to the tip of Cape Lookout is the chance to spot whales—motivation enough for some children. Cape Lookout is one of the best whale-watching sites on the Oregon Coast, and with more than two hundred gray whales now summering off Oregon, the chances of spotting a whale in midsummer aren't bad. Unfortunately, the best times are when the trail is at its muddiest: mid-March, during the northward migration, and December through early January, when the migrants are headed south to Baja for the winter. At those times, an average of fifteen to thirty whales may pass by in an hour.

Even if whales aren't sighted, the hike itself is worthwhile. Take it slow and easy, enjoying the views and the forest along the way. After the hike, drive south to Pacific City and look north at the long headland sticking way out from the mainland to see what you have just accomplished.

Two trails start side by side at the west end of the parking area. The trail on the right leads north 2.5 miles to the park's campground. Instead, take the left-hand trail. In about 75 yards go straight where another trail comes in from the left (it leads 2 miles down to the beach).

The terrain that the trail follows to the cape tip is rolling, but mostly slowly descending. At 0.6 mile the forest opens up to grand views of the beach and headlands to the south. From here, watch on the right for a plaque memorializing the victims of a 1943 plane crash. At 1.2 miles—about the halfway point—the trail reaches a fenced cliff on the north side of the cape, granting views of Oceanside and Three Arch Rocks.

The route winds back to the cape's south side, teasing hikers on with occasional views. A single strand of wire cable strung along the cliff does little more than warn hikers to take care; children may not get the hint, so watch them here. While approaching the tip, kids can listen for the buoy anchored offshore, moaning with the rhythm of the swells. Once they spot it, it's just a few more minutes' walk to the rocky point at the trail's end. Carry a picnic and binoculars and plan to linger awhile if you want to spot any whales, as the whales travel on their own schedule. Return as you came.

 WHALEN ISLAND

BEFORE YOU GO
For current conditions and more information, contact Clay Meyers State Natural Area at Whalen Island, *www.oregonstateparks.org* or (800) 551-6949

ABOUT THE HIKE
Day hike
Easy for children
1.5-mile loop
Nearly level
High point 10 feet
Hikable year-round

GETTING THERE

- From the stop light in the middle of Pacific City, turn west, following signs to Three Capes Loop
- Cross the river and turn north (becomes Sandlake Road)
- Drive 5.5 miles total from Pacific City to the sign to Whalen Island
- Turn left, cross the bridge over the estuary, and bear right into Clay Meyers State Natural Area at Whalen Island

HIKING THE TRAIL

Sand Lake is really a shallow bay—an estuary where freshwater and saltwater meet, nurturing a wide variety of marine plants and animals, from clams to salmon. In the middle of it is mile-long Whalen Island, with densely forested uplands in its middle descending to tidal mudflats all around. The island is a relatively recent addition to the state park system. The trail that now circles the island just above the high tide line takes you through a variety of habitats, to glimpses of the estuary and to the sandy beach on the island's west side.

From the parking area, take the trail north, bearing left where a spur trail on the right leads to an overlook at the edge of the estuary. The main trail stays just inside the forest's edge most of the way, rising toward the island's north end, where views open up of the water and hills to the north. The trail then curves south, following the island's ocean side and offering opportunities to detour onto the narrow sandy beach here, especially at the island's south end. Nearing the trailhead the loop trail meets the gravel wheelchair-accessible path from the parking lot at a viewpoint overlooking Sand Lake. Follow it back to the parking lot, bearing left at the spur trail leading to Whalen Island County Park, a rustic campground adjacent to the state natural area.

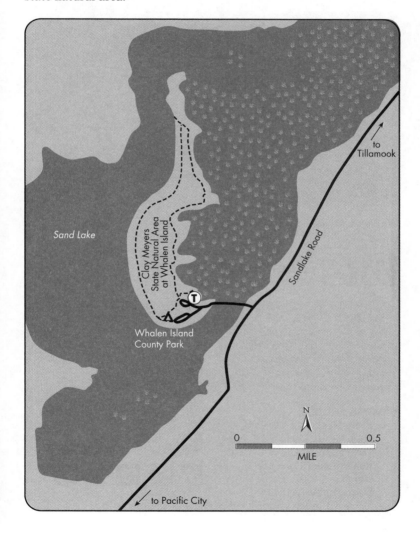

Whalen Island loop trail

HARTS COVE

BEFORE YOU GO
For current conditions and more information, contact Hebo Ranger District, *www.fs.fed.us /r6/siuslaw* or (503) 392-3161

ABOUT THE HIKE
Day hike or backpack
Challenging for children
5.8 miles round trip
800 feet elevation gain
High point 960 feet
Hikable mid-July through December
FYI Road 1861 to the trailhead is closed Jan. 1 through July 16

GETTING THERE
- From Neskowin take US Highway 101 south 3.6 miles
- Turn right on Cascade Head Road (Forest Road 1861), which is 4 miles north of State Highway 18
- Drive 4.1 miles to trailhead parking at the road's end

HIKING THE TRAIL

The hike to Harts Cove is more like a mountain hike than a beach hike, traversing deep forest and offering only occasional, distant ocean views. The hike doesn't go up a high headland or down to a secluded beach, but leads to a grassy slope overlooking a dramatic and remote stretch of coastline. On the way the trail winds through a magnificent hemlock and Sitka spruce forest and crosses a couple of rushing streams on footbridges. Most of the elevation loss (and on the return, gain) is in the first mile; after that, it's a pleasant stroll.

The trail drops quickly, steeply at times, switchbacking down the hill until it reaches a footbridge across Cliff Creek at 1 mile. Cross the creek, its bank lush with wildflowers in the spring. From here the trail climbs gently; listen for the sounds of birds and the rush of the creek, slowly fading. At about 1.5 miles you will hear the crash of waves on the cliffs below; beginning in October, the loud barking of California sea lions fills the air as well.

Shortly a sign announces the Neskowin Crest Research Natural Area and suggests looking around at the remains of 250-year-old Sitka spruce that have survived fires that destroyed other trees in the forest. Just beyond the sign is a bench offering the first view of Harts Cove.

The cove looks so close—but it's still a good mile away by trail. Follow the trail back up a ravine, across Chitwood Creek, then back through the loveliest, quietest, most magnificent old-growth forest yet seen along the trail. At 2.7 miles the trail emerges from the forest near the top of the grassy slope that overlooks Harts Cove to the south. Walk down the slope another 0.2 mile to peek down at the cove. There's a lot of room to play and explore without getting too close to the cliffs, but adults will want to watch children carefully just the same. There is no access down to (or, more to the point, back out of) Harts Cove. Return as you came.

Harts Cove

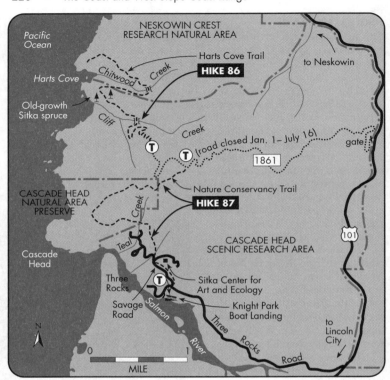

87 CASCADE HEAD

BEFORE YOU GO
For current conditions and more information, contact The Nature Conservancy, *www.thenatureconservancy.org* or (503) 230-1221

ABOUT THE HIKE
Day hike
Moderate for children
3.6 miles round trip
210 feet elevation gain
High point 330 feet
Hikable year-round
FYI no dogs allowed

GETTING THERE
■ From the junction of State Highway 18 and US Highway 101, take US 101 north 1.3 miles

- Turn west onto Three Rocks Road and drive 2.5 miles
- Just past Savage Road, turn left to parking at Knight Park Boat Landing

HIKING THE TRAIL

The hike to the grassy tip of Cascade Head traverses lovely woods and crosses boisterous creeks. But it's the view at the end—of the Salmon River estuary and coastline to the south—that makes this hike so memorable. A visit late or early in the day may reward hikers with views of deer grazing on the headland's open slopes.

The most popular trail on Cascade Head is the southern route to the headland's tip. From Knight Park walk back up Three Rocks Road to Savage Road, watching for a boardwalk on the right signaling the start of a little access trail. Follow it 0.4 mile to the Sitka Center road and continue on Savage Road a short distance to resumption of the trail (**Caution:** roadside parking here is minimal; there is no real shoulder). The trail starts up a steep hillside for the first 0.5 mile, then levels off, crossing several small creeks on wooden footbridges and boardwalks. Gently ascending, the trail follows the hillside's contours through the forest, emerging onto the open prairie a short walk from the south viewpoint, near a line of fencing beyond which hiking is prohibited. Return as you came, unless you're in the mood for some anaerobic exercise in the form of a steep climb to the summit knoll, another 0.7 mile and 880 feet straight up. The trail continues another mile to the north trailhead (3.5 miles one way), accessible from Forest Road 1861 mid-July through December (see Hike 86).

View south from Cascade Head

The trail out to Cascade Head passes through a 300-acre preserve owned and managed by The Nature Conservancy since 1966. Though the preserve is open to the public, the conservancy is rightfully protective of this seaside gem. Be extra careful to leave no trace here. In addition to using ordinary trail etiquette (don't litter, don't pick any vegetation), leave your dog at home and walk only on the trail. Certainly don't camp or build a fire on the headland.

 DRIFT CREEK FALLS

BEFORE YOU GO
For current conditions and more information, contact Hebo Ranger District, *www.fs.fed.us /r6/siuslaw* or (503) 392-3161

ABOUT THE HIKE
Day hike
Moderate for children
3.2 to 3.5 miles round trip
280 feet elevation gain
High point 910 feet
Hikable year-round

GETTING THERE
- From US Highway 101 at the south end of Lincoln City, 1 mile north of the Siletz River bridge, turn east onto Drift Creek Road

- Drive 1.6 miles and bear right onto South Drift Creek Road
- Drive 0.4 mile and veer left at the sign to Drift Creek Falls Trail (Forest Road 17)
- Drive 0.9 mile and turn left again
- Drive 3.3 miles and turn left at the fork
- Drive 0.6 mile and turn left again
- Drive 5.6 miles more to the trailhead parking area on the right
- Alternately, from State Highway 18 at Rose Lodge (just west of milepost 5), turn south onto Bear Creek Road
- Follow the main road (becomes FR 17), bearing right at the fork at 4.6 miles, to the trailhead in 9 miles

HIKING THE TRAIL
It's named for the dramatic waterfall that cascades 75 feet into a pool in Drift Creek. But it's the suspension bridge near the trail's end that catches the most attention on this hike. It hangs between support towers, each 29 feet tall, and is anchored to the bedrock on either side of Drift Creek. From the middle of the bridge you get a good look at the falls—if you dare; its gentle swaying motion can be a bit unnerving. It's a great hike for children with self-control and a well-developed sense of adventure—not for daredevils.

The hike to the falls descends gently, mainly through former clearcuts

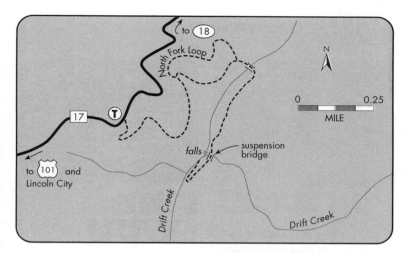

now growing trees ranging from ten to fifty years old, plus a narrow band of old growth. You'll pass a bench at 0.5 mile, then at 0.7 mile a junction with North Fork Trail on the left. Continuing on the main trail, you'll pass the other end of North Fork Loop and, at 1 mile, cross a small footbridge over a creek. At 1.25 miles the trail reaches the suspension bridge overlooking the falls. To reach the trail's end, cross the bridge and follow the trail's switchbacks down 0.25 mile, dropping 100 feet in elevation to the creek's edge.

Return as you came, or lengthen the hike a bit with a detour on the North Fork Loop, which winds up through a magnificent stand of century-old trees. The loop ascends, steeply in places, before leveling off and dropping to meet the main trail. Follow the main trail back to where you started.

Drift Creek Falls and suspension bridge

CAPE PERPETUA

BEFORE YOU GO
For current conditions and more information, contact Cape Perpetua Scenic Area, *www.fs.fed.us/r6/siuslaw* or (541) 547-3289

ABOUT THE HIKE
Day hike
Easy to moderate for children
0.4 to 2 miles round trip
Nearly level to 680 feet elevation gain
High point 800 feet
Hikable year-round

GETTING THERE
- From Yachats, drive south about 3 miles on US Highway 101
- Turn east at the sign to the Cape Perpetua Interpretive Center

HIKING THE TRAIL
From a sweet cove beach with blowholes and tide pools at either end to the steep, forested headland towering above, Cape Perpetua Scenic Area offers plenty of options to hikers of all ages and energy levels. These three are good starting points with children; check at the interpretive center here for information on longer hikes into the forest.

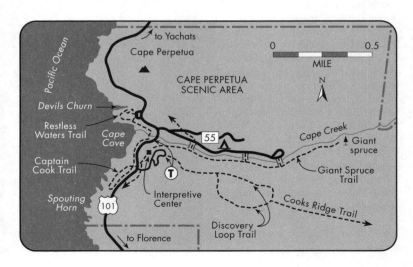

Rocks at Devils Churn

SHORELINE LOOP (1.3 MILES ROUND TRIP, MOSTLY LEVEL)

Link Captain Cook Trail with Restless Waters Trail for a scenic loop above the coastline. You could actually start at any of several pullouts along the highway and find your own way onto the loop. From the Interpretive Center, follow signs down a trail heading west, under the highway. At the end of the pedestrian tunnel, turn left and walk toward Spouting Horn, a hole in the top of a sea cave that spouts air and water when incoming waves build pressure inside the cave. Continue around to the south to do some tide pooling, if the tide is low enough. Return to the junction to continue the loop. Along the way, notice the mounds on the bluff above the beach. They're Indian middens—essentially garbage dumps—used by the Alsi Indians between about a.d. 600–1620. Archeologists believe the Alsi camped here in the summer while collecting mussels and other shellfish to eat.

From the tunnel, head north to reach Cape Cove Beach (look for a little spur trail leading to the beach on the south side of Cape Creek) and eventually Devils Churn. There you'll find a dead-end rock chute where waves race in and, at higher tide, crash dramatically, drenching visitors who stand too close. It was formed over thousands of years through the slow process of erosion; a crack in the basalt slab at the sea's edge was slowly worn into the chute you see today by the pounding of zillions of waves.

Spur trails loop back up to the highway at several spots, but you can follow the trail as far as curiosity leads, then return roughly as you came.

GIANT SPRUCE TRAIL (0.4 TO 2 MILES ROUND TRIP, NEARLY LEVEL)

The destination on this short, level hike is a 500-year-old Sitka spruce that kids can crawl under, thanks apparently to its having sprouted on a nurse log that's long since decayed and disappeared. The hike is ideal for preschoolers or for anyone looking for a short, leg-stretching outing along the coast. From the Interpretive Center, follow signs onto a paved path heading north toward Cape Creek. The path reaches a footbridge at 0.2 mile, but rather than crossing into the Cape Perpetua Campground, continue east another 0.6 mile along the musical creek's south bank to a footbridge at the end of the campground. (For an even shorter hike, drive to this point and start here.) From the footbridge it's a mostly level, 0.2-mile stretch to the giant spruce. The famed tree is about 15 feet in diameter and was 225 feet tall—until a 1962 windstorm snapped off its upper 35 feet.

DISCOVERY LOOP (2 MILES ROUND TRIP, 680 FEET ELEVATION GAIN)

For a short forest hike, head up Cooks Ridge Trail, which starts at the upper end of the parking lot above the Interpretive Center. The trail begins in dense Douglas fir and spruce and then leads into a lovely stand of old-growth Sitka spruce at about 0.7 mile, where a junction signals the start of a 0.6-mile midtrail loop. Hike the loop and return as you came for a 2-mile round trip. More energetic hikers could continue beyond the loop, which slowly ascends Cooks Ridge to link with other forest trails.

SHELL MIDDENS: ANCIENT GARBAGE DUMPS

On some beaches, such as the beach at Cape Perpetua (Hike 89) you may come across eroding bluffs that seem to be made not of sand or rock but of shells. These are probably middens, or refuse heaps left by long-ago inhabitants. By studying middens, archaeologists glean clues about the lives of people who lived on the Oregon coast in prehistoric times. Identification of the shells and bones in a midden reveal some of the foods people ate. Sometimes scientists find objects of daily living such as discarded tools made from stone, shell, and bone. By analyzing the size of middens, they gain clues to how long people occupied the site. The oldest known human settlement on the Oregon coast, near Bandon, is about 10,000 years old.

 HOBBIT BEACH–CHINA CREEK

BEFORE YOU GO
For current conditions and more information, contact Carl G. Washburne Memorial State Park, www.oregonstateparks.org or (800) 551-6949

ABOUT THE HIKE
Day hike
Easy to moderate for children
0.5 to 4.75 miles round trip
Up to 200 feet elevation gain
High point 200 feet
Hikable year-round

GETTING THERE
- From Florence, follow US Highway 101 north about 12 miles

- Look for parking on the east side of the highway and the signed trailhead on the west side of the highway as the highway flattens and straightens
- Trailhead is 1.2 miles south of the entrance to Carl G. Washburne State Park and/or 0.8 mile north of the entrance to Heceta Head Lighthouse State Scenic Viewpoint

HIKING THE TRAIL
What would a hobbit's trail look like? It would most likely be hidden, a little tunnel through deep woods, with fantastical, moss-covered trees. It

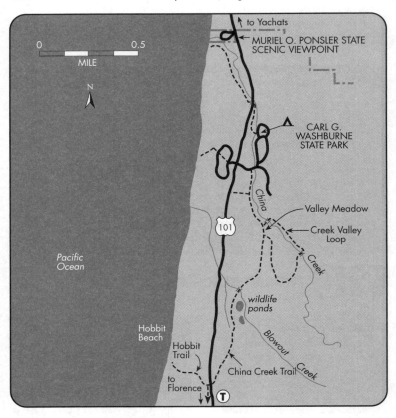

might even be a little spooky, and it should definitely lead to a magical place. Certainly the Hobbit Trail fits that description. Take it to Hobbit Beach, or follow the China Creek Trail into the forest east of the highway for wonderful woods walking and picnicking along the shallow creek.

HOBBIT BEACH (0.5 MILE ROUND TRIP, 200 FEET ELEVATION GAIN)

The trail begins at a wooden trail post on the west side of the highway. Cars zoom by pretty fast here; watch kids carefully while lacing shoes and loading packs. From the trailhead go west, continuing straight at the junction (a left turn leads to Heceta Head Lighthouse). The path winds through a forest of pines and spruce and tall rhododendrons, twisting downhill 0.25 mile. It's easy to imagine running into a hobbit scurrying along this trail—or to imagine you are one yourself. Approaching the beach, the trail drops into a narrow sand chute, with salal closing in overhead. Suddenly you're on the beach just north of the massive Heceta Head. Return as you came, or link with China Creek Trail for a longer loop (see below).

CHINA CREEK LOOP (3.4 TO 4.75 MILES ROUND TRIP, 120 TO 200 FEET ELEVATION GAIN)

Often overlooked in favor of the Hobbit Trail, this trail winds through the gorgeous coastal forest east of the highway on either side of China Creek, south of the campground at Carl G. Washburne State Park. From the parking turnout on the highway's east side, the trail drops down briefly, then levels off, following the route of the old coast highway north along slow-moving Blowout Creek. At 0.5 mile the trail passes a couple of ponds; look for evidence of beavers. It crosses a creek and then continues north through the woods. A few steps before the trail emerges from the trees and drops down into sunny Valley Meadow at 1.3 miles, you'll reach a spur trail to the right. Take it, crossing a small creek on a culvert. The trail heads up briefly, then zigzags south and east across a carpet of moss, to the accompaniment of the ocean's roar. It drops down and veers north, crossing a footbridge at babbling China Creek at 0.5 mile, then follows the creek's east bank to a second footbridge at Valley Meadow 0.75 mile after leaving the main trail. Return to the main trail and follow it south back to your starting point.

For a longer loop hike, continue north from Valley Meadow on the main trail into the park's campground, picking up a trail to the beach

Trail to Hobbit Beach

238 = The Coast and West Slope Coast Range

at the campground's far end and following it to the beach. Walk the beach south to Hobbit Beach and return to your car via the Hobbit Trail (total loop: 4.75 miles). Shorten the loop to 3.75 miles by walking out the campground entrance road, crossing the highway, and accessing the beach via the highway rest area.

 KENTUCKY FALLS

BEFORE YOU GO
For current conditions and more information, contact Mapleton Ranger District, *www.fs.fed.us/r6/siuslaw* or (541) 902-8526

ABOUT THE HIKE
Day hike
Moderate for children
3.6 miles round trip
760 feet elevation gain
High point 1560 feet
Hikable most of the year

GETTING THERE
- From Eugene, take State Highway 126 west about 35 miles
- Between mileposts 26 and 27, turn south at the sign to Clay Creek and Whittaker Creek Recreation Site
- Drive 1.5 miles
- Turn right and drive another 1.5 miles
- Bear left on Dunn Ridge Road and drive 7 miles

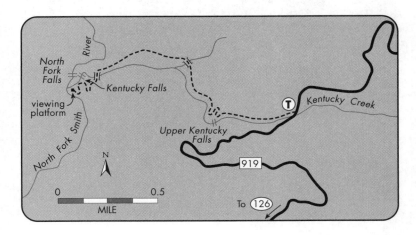

- Turn left, following a sign to Reedsport (road turns to gravel) and drive 2.8 miles
- Turn right onto Forest Road 23 and drive 1.6 miles
- Turn right onto Forest Road 919 (gravel ends) and continue 2.7 miles to the trailhead.

HIKING THE TRAIL

It's necessary to drive a bit to get to the trailhead for Kentucky Falls, but it's worth it. The hike in is easy—almost too easy—and the mostly downhill trail ends at a pair of side-by-side waterfalls at the confluence of two creeks. Winter rains swell the falls, adding to their drama. Though the trail is snow-free virtually all year, snow sometimes blocks the road around 2862-foot Roman Nose Mountain; in winter, call the Mapleton Ranger District for road conditions.

Follow the trail into gorgeous old-growth and second-growth forest, listening for bird songs and looking for wildflowers in spring. After about 0.6 mile of fairly level walking, you'll reach a viewpoint overlooking Upper Kentucky Falls. The trail then drops quickly to the falls' base.

The trail follows Kentucky Creek then winds away from it a short distance to cross a side creek on a railed log bridge at 1.4 miles. For the last 0.4 mile the trail switchbacks steadily into the canyon, signaling to children that they're nearing the end (and that they'd better steel themselves for the return hike).

At the trail's end, you will see both the North Fork Smith River and Kentucky Creek cascading down a cliff just upstream of the two creeks' confluence. A wooden viewing platform at the end covers a tangle of boulders that used to make viewing the falls a dangerous proposition for all but the most nimble-footed; now it's quite safe. Explore around the base of the falls a bit before turning around and tackling the return trip.

Kentucky Falls

92 SWEET CREEK

BEFORE YOU GO
For current conditions and more information, contact Mapleton Ranger District, www.fs.fed.us/r6/siuslaw or (541) 902-8526

ABOUT THE HIKE
Day hike
Moderate for children
3 miles one way
480 feet elevation gain
High point 600 feet
Hikable year-round

GETTING THERE

- From Florence, take State Highway 126 east 14 miles to the Siuslaw River Bridge in Mapleton
- At the east end of the bridge, turn south on Sweet Creek Road (County Road 48)
- Drive 11 miles
- Park at the Homestead Trailhead, on the right

HIKING THE TRAIL

Visit in winter, when the creek is full and the falls roar over bedrock ledges. Better yet, visit in midsummer to wade across those ledges, splash in shallow pools, and savor the sun and dappled shade of this very sweet

Sweet Creek

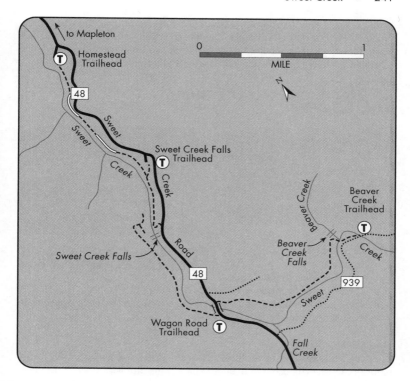

creek. Extensive boardwalks add to the fun of a kids' hike here. It's in the foothills of the Coast Range, about a half-hour from US Highway 101.

You can access four trailheads from Sweet Creek Road. Most hikers start at the first one, the Homestead Trailhead (the only one with a rest room). From here it's a bit more than 1 mile up the gorge by trail to one of the creek's main attractions, 90-foot Sweet Creek Falls. This trail section is especially appealing; where the creek gorge narrows, a railed catwalk hugs the cliff above the churning water. If this 1-mile trek is more hike than you want, drive 0.5 mile farther to the Sweet Creek Falls Trailhead. The falls are just 0.5 mile by trail from here. Spur trails on either side of the creek lead to views of water splashing down the basalt staircase.

Although the trail seems to end at the falls, in fact it resumes across the boulder-strewn creek. There's no footbridge, and a midwinter crossing on slick rocks isn't recommended with children. Agile, older children can manage the crossing in summer; look for the trail heading up the opposite bank and follow it to where it meets the road at a road bridge. (Or drive 0.75 mile farther to Wagon Road Trailhead, adjacent to the road bridge.) From this third trailhead it's 0.5 mile by trail to Beaver Creek Falls, where the main trail ends. The fourth trailhead, Beaver Creek, lies off a signed spur road (Forest Road 939) just up Road 48 and leads down a separate, short trail to a view of Beaver Falls from above.

 WAXMYRTLE TRAIL

BEFORE YOU GO
For current conditions and more information, contact Oregon Dunes National Recreation Area, www.fs.fed.us/r6 /siuslaw or (541) 271-3611

ABOUT THE HIKE
Day hike
Moderate for children
2.5 miles round trip
Nearly level
High point 40 feet
Hikable year-round

GETTING THERE
- From Florence take US Highway 101 south about 7 miles
- Turn west onto Siltcoos Beach Road
- Drive 1 mile, just beyond the entrance to Waxmyrtle Campground
- Park in the Stagecoach Trailhead parking area, on the left

HIKING THE TRAIL
This trail follows the meandering Siltcoos River for its last 1.25 miles before reaching the ocean. It's short enough for almost any child to hike, and the ever-present opportunity to see wild birds on or near the river entertains kids as they walk. Changing views also keep things interesting along the way. At the end, there's the beach. Be sure to pack in a kite!

On foot, backtrack 0.1 mile on the trail to the Waxmyrtle Campground road, cross the Siltcoos River, and turn west where the trail begins following the river's south bank. Climb stairs up a short hill forested with shore pines, continuing along the bluff. At 0.4 mile there's a junction. Bear right on the "Estuary Trail" and you'll follow a riverside route out to the beach (may be difficult at high tide). This is a good stretch for seeing cormorants, kingfishers, great blue herons, and other water-loving birds. It is closed September 15 to March 15 to protect nesting plovers; in winter, when it's open, dogs must be on leash.

Otherwise, at the junction with the Estuary Trail, bear left on "Beach Access Trail" leading onto an old sand road; 0.4 mile from the junction you'll reach Waxmyrtle Marsh, on the left. The marsh is an old channel of the Siltcoos River that was cut off over time; water birds visit throughout the year, and beaver and nutria live here as well. Continue another 0.25 mile to the beach. Return as you came, or—in fall or winter, and if tide permits—loop around to return on the Estuary Trail.

Extend your outing with a walk on 1-mile River of No Return Loop Trail, which follows an old arm of the Siltcoos River around Lagoon Campground on a combination of boardwalk and footpath. It starts just across Siltcoos Beach Road from the Stagecoach Trailhead.

HELPING TO BRING BACK THE SNOWY PLOVER

If you visit the beach between mid-March and mid-September, especially near creek mouths such as on Hike 93 or 94, you may see signs and fences blocking access to the dry sand. It's all to protect the snowy plover. Unlike other shorebirds, this small bird nests on flat, open sandy beaches at the high-tide line. This makes it vulnerable to predators (and to disturbance by humans and their pets). Development of the shoreline has reduced the birds' habitat, so that it is now considered a threatened species. You can help restore the plover population by observing the signs and avoiding prime nesting habitat spring through fall.

Waxmyrtle Trail

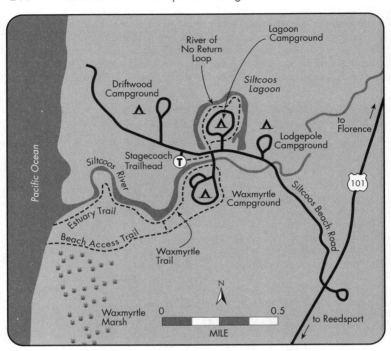

94 OREGON DUNES OVERLOOK

BEFORE YOU GO
For current conditions and more information, contact Oregon Dunes National Recreation Area, www.fs.fed.us/r6 /siuslaw or (541) 271-3611

ABOUT THE HIKE
Day hike
Moderate for children
2 miles round trip; 3.3-mile loop
Up to 300 feet elevation gain
High point 140 feet
Hikable year-round

GETTING THERE
- From Florence, follow US Highway 101 south about 10 miles
- Alternately, drive about the same distance north from Reedsport
- Turn west at the sign to Oregon Dunes day-use area

HIKING THE TRAIL

The overlook at Oregon Dunes day-use area was built to give motorists a taste of the dunes on a quick detour off US Highway 101. It's also the trailhead for a wonderfully varied loop hike that takes in open dunes, the ocean beach, tree islands, and coastal forest. Though there's not much elevation gain, it's more difficult than forest hikes of comparable distance because much of the walking is on soft sand. Post-to-post routefinding across the shifting dunes adds an element of adventure.

ROUND TRIP TO THE BEACH (2 MILES, 140 FEET ELEVATION GAIN)

You can reach the main beach trail from one of two directions: either walk down a winding, sandy trail from the upper viewing deck, or follow the long switchbacks on the trail leading down the hill from the main covered viewing structure adjacent to the parking lot. Both approaches take you to the middle of an open dune; from here, posts mark the route west across about 0.3 mile of open sand. To reach the beach, bear right with the posts to enter the deflation plain, which the trail crosses with help from small bridges. Climbing over the foredune, the trail reaches the beach at 1 mile.

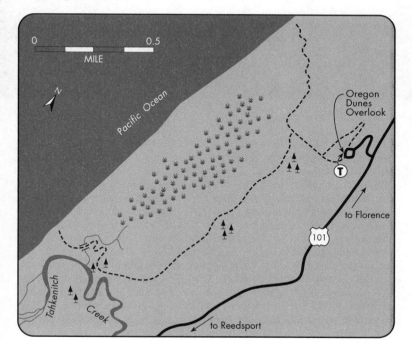

Oregon Dunes Overlook loop trail

BEACH TRAIL LOOP (3.3 MILES, 300 FEET ELEVATION GAIN)

For a loop hike, take the beach trail, then walk south along the beach for 1.5 miles until you see a trail post in the foredune (if you reach Tahkenitch Creek, you've gone too far). The trail leads up and over the foredune, granting a glimpse of Tahkenitch Creek on the right; pause to look for ospreys and bald eagles. Cross a little footbridge 0.2 mile from the beach, then head up into a tall "island" of shore pines. From the summit you'll again see the creek. Drop down the other side of the tree island and begin trekking across a Sahara-like landscape of open dunes, following marker posts leading to another tree island. Follow the trail around the tree island's west side, then get back on the open sand. The trail skirts west of the next big tree island. (Look carefully for the post here; it's deeply buried in sand and hard to spot.) Just before reaching the end of the loop in the open sand below the overlook, the trail enters the deflation plain and becomes a narrow, sandy path.

JOHN DELLENBACK TRAIL

BEFORE YOU GO
For current conditions and more information, contact Oregon Dunes National Recreation Area, *www.fs.fed.us/r6/siuslaw* or (541) 271-3611

ABOUT THE HIKE
Day hike
Challenging for children
5 miles round trip
120 feet elevation gain
High point 120 feet
Hikable year-round

GETTING THERE
- From Reedsport, take US Highway 101 south about 8 miles
- Alternately, drive north about 12 miles from North Bend
- Just south of Eel Creek Campground, look for the signed trailhead parking area

HIKING THE TRAIL
The most adventurous and challenging of all the trails in Oregon Dunes National Recreation Area is the walk on John Dellenback Trail across Umpqua Dunes to the beach. It's perhaps too adventurous for many children; others (older, more determined) will find it thrilling, certainly doable if you take it slow and pick a good weather day. It begins on an easy 1-mile interpretive loop trail that any child could handle, with a spur to campsites at Eel Creek Campground. Then the loop trail ends and the real adventure begins: crossing the widest swath of open dunes in the entire Oregon Dunes, with help from a few widely scattered wooden posts.

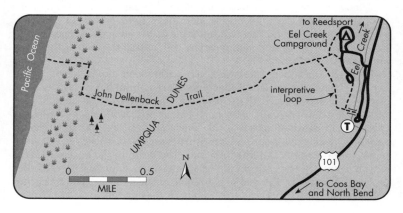

Umpqua Dunes

Hikers need to stay on their toes and do a little common-sense orienteering to get back to where they started. The elevation figure listed with the hike is just the rise from the parking lot to the edge of the open dunes; you could easily quadruple that figure hiking up and down the open dunes on the way to the beach. This hike is no fun on a wet or windy day.

A long footbridge immediately crosses Eel Creek and leads to a junction, the start of the interpretive loop. Bear right or left; either way will lead you up and around to a tall dune at the edge of the open sand. Enjoy some climbing and sliding before completing the loop, if that's as much as you want to tackle.

To reach the beach, head west across the open dunes, keeping the big tree island on your left. Wooden posts are helpful but not really necessary. When you reach the end of the open sand at the edge of the vegetated deflation plain, turn north; signs will lead you to the start of a trail through the marsh to the beach. Most of the year this trail is very soggy; consider wearing waterproof sandals, because you're going to get wet. Cross the tall foredune and drop down to the beach. Return as you came. On the return trip across the open sand, aim toward the blue water tower in the distance to land in the general vicinity of the interpretive trail, which will lead you back to your car.

TREE ISLANDS AND TRANSITION FORESTS

The 1-mile-wide plant community found between the Oregon Dunes and the forest stretching up into the Coast Range is a unique mix of trees including Sitka spruce, western hemlock, Douglas fir, and shore pine. Shore pine grows right on the coast but not in the Coast Range forest. Sitka spruce does, but only two to three miles inland (though it grows as much as 100 miles up the Columbia River). You'll also find huge rhododendron, evergreen huckleberry, and salmonberry growing here. Over time, shifting sands sometimes isolate patches of forest to create "tree islands": steep-sloped miniforests surrounded by open dunes.

96 CAPE ARAGO

BEFORE YOU GO
For current conditions and more information, contact Sunset Bay State Park, *www .oregonstateparks.org* or (800) 551-6949

ABOUT THE HIKE
Day hike
Moderate for children
3.5 miles one way
120 feet elevation gain
High point 120 feet
Hikable year-round

GETTING THERE

- From US Highway 101 in North Bend or Coos Bay, follow signs about 8 miles southwest to the town of Charleston
- Take Cape Arago Highway south about 5 miles to Sunset Bay State Park

- Park near the rest rooms at the south end of the park
- Southern trailhead is at viewpoint 3 miles farther south (0.5 mile north of road's end)

HIKING THE TRAIL

Three contiguous state parks south of Charleston offer diverse opportunities to families, including swimming (or wading) in a protected cove, strolling through formal gardens, and picnicking on a bluff overlooking the Pacific. What most visitors to this area never see, however, is the dramatic, rocky shoreline that's only accessible by trail. So pull on some boots (it's muddy in places) and walk part or all of the Oregon Coast Trail between Sunset Bay State Park, Shore Acres State Park,

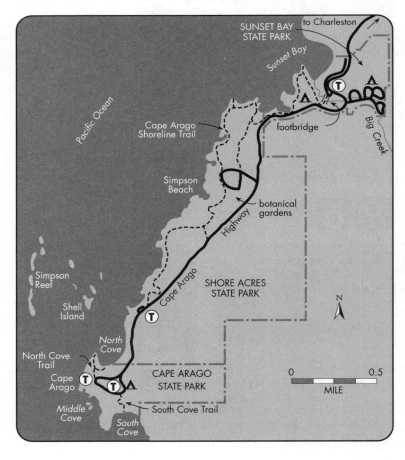

Shoreline between Sunset Bay and Shore Acres

and the viewpoint 0.5 mile north of Cape Arago. Hike as a one-way trek with a shuttle car, or consider a round-trip hike from, say, Sunset Bay to Shore Acres (3.6 miles).

Look for a trail post near the rest rooms at the south end of the Sunset Bay State Park parking area. Cross the footbridge over Big Creek, ascend the headland, and bear right around a big mowed meadow, then continue south along the bluff. At 0.6 mile the trail leads back out to the highway, follows it south a short distance, and resumes at a stile over the guardrail. It continues through woods some distance from the shoreline; at a junction, veer north and west out to the bluff, where you'll view the lighthouse to the north and rocks to the south (or continue straight for a shortcut through the forest to Shore Acres State Park).

Approaching Shore Acres at about 1.8 miles, either detour east and enter the botanical gardens (exiting through the open gate at the back of the gardens, where you can pick up the trail again) or follow a trail winding to the west of the gardens. In either case, stick to the paved paths to avoid confusion. From Shore Acres the trail leads down to intimate Simpson Beach, into woods, and then back up onto a bluff. At the trail junction, bear right. (A left turn leads to the highway.) The trail leads out to the shore, back to the highway briefly at 3.3 miles, resumes as trail, and ends at a viewpoint overlooking Shell Island, 0.5 mile north of the road's end at Cape Arago State Park. Bring binoculars for the best views of the sea lions, harbor seals, and elephant seals seen on the island at various seasons.

From the Cape Arago State Park parking loop at the end of the highway, you can follow trails 0.2 mile down to the cape's North Cove (closed March 1 through July 1) or South Cove (open year-round) for tide pooling, wildlife watching, and beach playing.

 SOUTH SLOUGH

BEFORE YOU GO
For current conditions and more information, contact South Slough National Estuarine Research Reserve, www.oregon.gov/dsl/ssnerr or (541) 888-5558

ABOUT THE HIKE
Day hike
Easy to moderate for children
0.5 to 3 miles round trip
Up to 320 feet elevation gain
High point 320 feet
Hikable year-round

GETTING THERE
- From US Highway 101 in North Bend or Coos Bay, follow signs about 8 miles southwest to the town of Charleston
- Turn south on Seven Devils Road at the sign to South Slough
- Drive 4.3 miles to the signed entrance to the research reserve, on the left
- The interpretive center trailhead is straight ahead
- Hidden Creek Trailhead is down a 0.2-mile spur road to the right
- Big Cedar Trailhead is a 0.2-mile walk past locked gate on the road from the Hidden Creek Trailhead (or get key at interpretive center)

HIKING THE TRAIL
The South Slough of Coos Bay was designated a national estuarine reserve in 1974 to preserve this relatively complete estuarine system for study and recreation. Three trails lead to a two-level viewing platform alongside the estuary, and from there to what's called Sloughside Pilings, where old dikes are slowly being reclaimed by the tides. Among those three trails, Big Cedar Trail is the shortest and easiest, built to accommodate wheelchairs; disabled visitors may stop at the interpretive center and pick up a key to the locked gate on the access road (call ahead). Hidden Creek is the most popular; it follows the tripping creek to a boardwalk through a skunk cabbage bog. The trail from the interpretive center is the longest and steepest. Begin your visit with a stop at the interpretive center, if it's open, where displays geared for children help orient youngsters for what they'll see on the hike.

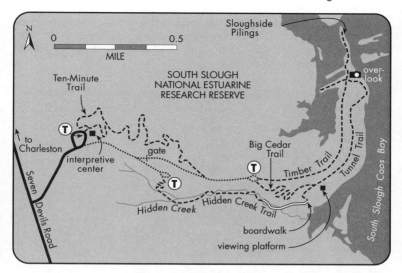

BIG CEDAR TRAIL (0.5 MILES ROUND TRIP, NEARLY LEVEL)

Two trails start at the trailhead; take the right-hand trail and follow a gently descending route on gravel path and curving wooden boardwalk 0.5 mile to the viewing platform.

HIDDEN CREEK TRAIL (2.5 MILES ROUND TRIP, 180 FEET ELEVATION GAIN)

From the Hidden Creek Trailhead, drop down the hillside, crossing and recrossing Hidden Creek as it flows to the slough. At sea level, a long, wooden boardwalk leads through a skunk cabbage bog, odorous and bright yellow in early spring, even in late winter. The route skirts a corner of the salt marsh and then makes a brief zigzag ascent to the viewing platform.

INTERPRETIVE CENTER TRAIL (3 MILES ROUND TRIP, 320 FEET ELEVATION GAIN)

Begin hiking the Ten-Minute Trail, but leave the loop and follow the trail down the hill. At 0.4 mile the trail reaches gravel Big Cedar Trail access road; cross it to pick up Hidden Creek Trail or follow the road down 0.1 mile to pick up the Big Cedar Trail to the viewing platform.

From the viewing platform you can follow the Tunnel Trail to Sloughside Pilings (0.5 mile). The Tunnel Trail leads through dense forest, passes another overlook, and heads down steps approaching the edge of the water. Spur trails lead out along the marsh and onto old dikes. The dikes were built years ago by homesteaders reclaiming the marsh for pasture land. Now they're slowly crumbling, as the estuary returns to its natural state. Return to the viewing platform as you came, or take the Timber Trail—part footpath, part sand road—that gently winds back to the Big Cedar Trailhead.

WATCH YOUR STEP! CARNIVOROUS PLANTS

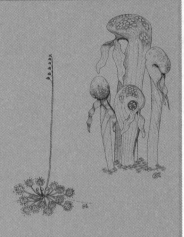

Actually, these plants won't harm you; both species of carnivorous plants found on the Oregon Coast stick to a diet of insects. Tiny sundew plants (*Drosera rotundifolia*) can be found near the dikes on the Tunnel Trail at South Slough (Hike 97). The end of the sundew's rounded leaf blades, fanned out close to the ground, are covered by fine hairs tipped with digestive glands. Insects get trapped in the hairs and consumed. The pitcher plant (*Darlingtonia californica*) also uses its purple-green leaves to lure, capture, and digest the insects it uses to supplement its diet. At six inches to three feet tall, it's much easier to spot, especially where it grows in crowded bogs such as at Darlingtonia State Natural Area, on the east side of US 101 a few miles north of Florence on the central coast.

Boardwalk at South Slough

PORT ORFORD HEADS

ABOUT THE HIKE
Day hike
Easy for children
0.6 mile round trip; 1.2-mile loop
100 feet elevation gain
High point 320 feet
Hikable year-round

GETTING THERE

- From US Highway 101 at the north end of Port Orford, turn west onto Ninth Street

- Follow signs onto Coast Guard Road and up the hill to the park's parking area

HIKING THE TRAIL

Port Orford Heads have some of the most stunning vistas on the entire coast. And from 1934 to 1970 those viewpoints had a very important practical purpose: to spot trouble at sea. The Port Orford Lifeboat Station housed as many as one hundred "surfmen" whose job it was to

Lifeboat on display at Port Orford Heads

keep watch over 40 miles of coastline and, when needed, dash down more than 530 steps to a boathouse in Nellies Cove and head out, often in huge storms, in unsinkable 36-foot motor lifeboats. (The surfmen's motto: "You have to go out; you don't have to come back.") Their observation tower, boathouse, and stairs are all gone, but you can see their remains and the dramatic vistas the surfmen surveyed on a loop hike at Port Orford Heads that starts at the old lifeboat station, now serving as Port Orford Lifeboat Station Museum and Interpretive Center (open Thursdays through Mondays, April through October).

An interconnected network of short trails starts at the center. It's just 0.6 mile straight out to the tower viewpoint and back, but in an easy loop of only 1.2 miles you can see several more viewpoints. From

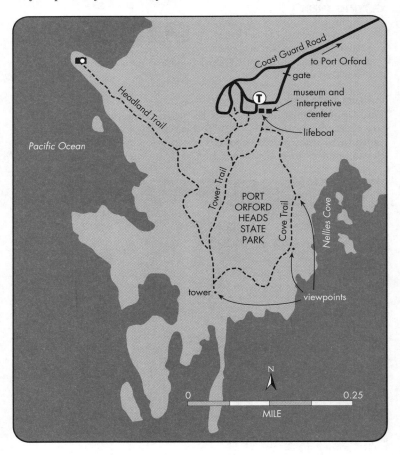

the shelter housing the restored lifeboat at the old lifeboat station, bear left to take the Cove Trail. Pausing at a view 280 feet down into Nellies Cove, look for the concrete breakwater and portions of the boathouse foundation and boat carriage rails, and peer back up the cliff to see foundations that once anchored the staircase. Soon you'll reach another great view of the coast and, at 0.4 mile, a dramatic view of Humbug Mountain from the site of the station's observation tower. To return, head inland and uphill on the Tower Trail, then bear left at two trail junctions to link with the Headland Trail, which leads to the park's westernmost viewpoint (watch for the flash from Cape Blanco Lookout). Returning, follow the Headland Trail a scant 0.2 mile and bear left to walk another 0.2 mile back to the parking area.

 HUMBUG MOUNTAIN

BEFORE YOU GO
For current conditions and more information, contact Humbug Mountain State Park, *www.oregonstateparks.org* or (800) 551-6949

ABOUT THE HIKE
Day hike
Challenging for children
5 to 6 miles round trip
1720 feet elevation gain
High point 1730 feet
Hikable year-round

GETTING THERE
- From Port Orford, take US Highway 101 south about 6 miles

- Look for the trailhead on the north side of US Highway 101, just west of the entrance to Humbug Mountain State Park Campground

HIKING THE TRAIL
I wouldn't have thought to recommend this fairly taxing hike for children—if I hadn't shared the summit views with a pair of youngsters who had beat me to the top. Forested Humbug Mountain dominates the south coast with its steep rise from tide pools to sky. In spring, wildflowers brighten the trailside and the creeks are raucous. In autumn, fallen bay leaves crunch underfoot, sending their spicy fragrance into the air. There isn't a season when the hike up Humbug Mountain isn't appealing.

Start at the trailhead along the highway, or take a short trail from the park campground across Brush Creek and under the highway. The summit trail immediately crosses a small creek and begins climbing through an airy forest of Douglas fir, rhododendrons, and bay trees;

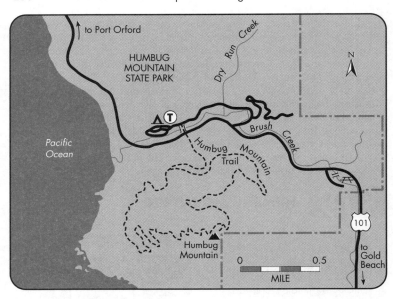

it continues up at a moderately steep grade.

Just past a 1-mile marker the trail splits. Bear left and it's another 2 miles to the summit; bear right and it's 1.5 miles to the same point. The 1.5-mile route reopened in 1993, twenty-five years after it was closed following a major blowdown of trees during the Northwest's infamous Columbus Day storm. Enjoy the views of the ocean and Port Orford on this stretch of trail. Just short of the summit the two approaches meet; follow the trail a few paces to the summit, where you can drink in the view to the south from a small, grassy clearing. Return as you came or loop back to the junction on the alternate trail.

Humbug Mountain Trail

REDWOOD NATURE TRAIL

BEFORE YOU GO
For current conditions and more information, contact Alfred A. Loeb State Park, *www.oregonstateparks.org* or (800) 551-6949

ABOUT THE HIKE
Day hike
Easy to moderate for children
1- to 2.5-mile loop
370 feet elevation gain
High point 470 feet
Hikable year-round

GETTING THERE
- In Brookings, just north of the Chetco River Bridge on US 101, turn east onto North Bank Road

- Drive 7.8 miles to the picnic area at Alfred A. Loeb State Park
- Continue 0.6 mile more to the start of the loop trail, on the left

HIKING THE TRAIL
There's something special about being in a redwood forest. The big trees with their reddish bark and lacy-needle boughs draping loftily overhead create a magical atmosphere. This trail is all the more fun because it's unexpected. First, redwoods are supposed to be in California, not

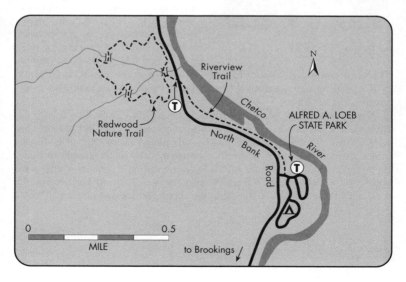

Redwood Nature Trail

Oregon. (These are actually the northernmost redwoods in the world.) Second, the lushness of the forest here, a few miles inland, contrasts sharply with the often-open headlands of the south coast for those traveling along US Highway 101. The hike is short, but there are some fairly steep stretches, making it feel more like a real hike than just a nature walk.

Starting at the main trailhead, pick up an interpretive pamphlet (if available) at the station by the rest room just up the trail. Shortly the trail reaches a junction; turn left to hike clockwise, following the order of numbered posts, which correspond with explanations in the trail pamphlet. The brochure focuses mostly on natural history but weaves in some human history as well; one post marks an old log-cage bear trap built years ago and long abandoned. For the first 0.5 mile, Douglas firs predominate along the trail as it ascends steadily. After crossing a footbridge over a creek, you'll start seeing big redwoods and a lot of rhododendrons. The trail peaks at about 0.75 mile. Cross the creek again, then start switchbacking down through the forest to recross the creek and meet the start of the loop.

For a longer hike, start at Alfred A. Loeb State Park. The 0.75-mile Riverview Trail begins in the park's picnic area, on the left side of the park entrance road. The trail mostly rolls along, in and out of leafy ravines, threading a narrow corridor between the Chetco River and the road. With wide gravel bars and a lazy current, the river is inviting in summer and easy to access from the trail, especially toward either end. It ends across the road from the main trailhead for Redwood Nature Trail.

INDEX

ABOUT THE AUTHOR

Bonnie Henderson grew up in Portland, Oregon, and spent most family vacations hiking and backpacking in Mount Hood National Forest. During college she began guiding white-water raft trips and leading teenagers on wilderness backpacking trips in the Rocky, Cascade, and Olympic Mountains, and later taught cross-country skiing at Mount St. Helens. She earned a master's degree in journalism and has since been a newspaper and magazine reporter and editor and a freelance writer. She lives in Eugene, Oregon, and enjoys hiking with her family and friends. Read about other books by Bonnie Henderson at *www.bonniehendersonwrites.com*.

Bonnie Henderson

THE MOUNTAINEERS, founded in 1906, is a nonprofit outdoor activity and conservation club, whose mission is "to explore, study, preserve, and enjoy the natural beauty of the outdoors. . . . " Based in Seattle, Washington, the club is now the third-largest such organization in the United States, with seven branches throughout Washington State.

The Mountaineers sponsors both classes and year-round outdoor activities in the Pacific Northwest, which include hiking, mountain climbing, ski-touring, snowshoeing, bicycling, camping, kayaking, nature study, sailing, and adventure travel. The club's conservation division supports environmental causes through educational activities, sponsoring legislation, and presenting informational programs.

All club activities are led by skilled, experienced instructors, who are dedicated to promoting safe and responsible enjoyment and preservation of the outdoors.

If you would like to participate in these organized outdoor activities or the club's programs, consider a membership in The Mountaineers. For information and an application, write or call The Mountaineers, Club Headquarters, 300 Third Avenue West, Seattle, WA 98119; 206-284-6310. You can also visit the club's website at www.mountaineers.org or contact The Mountaineers via email at clubmail@mountaineers.org.

The Mountaineers Books, an active, nonprofit publishing program of the club, produces guidebooks, instructional texts, historical works, natural history guides, and works on environmental conservation. All books produced by The Mountaineers Books fulfill the club's mission.

Send or call for our catalog of more than 500 outdoor titles:

The Mountaineers Books
1001 SW Klickitat Way, Suite 201
Seattle, WA 98134
800-553-4453
mbooks@mountaineersbooks.org
www.mountaineersbooks.org

The Mountaineers Books is proud to be a corporate sponsor of The Leave No Trace Center for Outdoor Ethics, whose mission is to promote and inspire responsible outdoor recreation through education, research, and partnerships. The Leave No Trace program is focused specifically on human-powered (nonmotorized) recreation.

Leave No Trace strives to educate visitors about the nature of their recreational impacts, as well as offer techniques to prevent and minimize such impacts. Leave No Trace is best understood as an educational and ethical program, not as a set of rules and regulations.

For more information, visit *www.LNT.org,* or call 800-332-4100.

OTHER TITLES YOU MIGHT ENJOY FROM THE MOUNTAINEERS BOOKS

100 Classic Hikes in Oregon
Douglas Lorain
Gorgeous guide to Oregon's most dramatic trails—suitable for coffee table treatment.

Best Hikes with Dogs: Oregon
Ellen Bishop
Dog-legal, dog-safe hikes guaranteed to delight masters and pet friends alike.

Best Short Hikes in Northwest Oregon
Rhonda and George Ostertag
Done-in-a-day hikes for nature lovers of all abilities.

Best Old-Growth Forest Hikes: Washington and Oregon Cascades
John and Diane Cissel
Hike among the ancients, and soak in what time has to offer.

Day Hiking: Oregon Coast
Bonnie Henderson
Beach walks are best—get all of them in this one book.

Hiking Oregon's Geology, 2nd Ed.
Ellen Morris Bishop & John Eliot Allen
Hikes with a point—understanding the geology under every place you step!

The Mountaineers Books has more than 500 outdoor recreation titles in print.
Receive a free catalog at
www.mountaineersbooks.org.